HEALING COMMUNICATION:

A Psychospiritual Approach

HEALING COMMUNICATION:

A Psychospiritual Approach

by
RICK PHILLIPS

DΞVA ✴ PUBLISHING
New Mexico, USA

Phillips, Rick.
　　Healing communication: a psychospiritual approach / by Rick Phillips
　　　p. cm.
　　　ISBN 978-0-9653059-0 : $12.00
　　　1. New Age　　2. Self-help　　3. Transpersonal Psychology

DEVA Foundation
P.O. Box 309
Glorieta, NM 87535
Tel/Fax 505-757-6752
http://www.deva.org

Cover photography: Rick Phillips
Cover Design: Bob Wartell
Editing: Ardis Burst & Brandt Morgan
Typography: Michael G. Brown

Printed in the USA by:
Bookcrafters, Chelsea, MI

ISBN 978-0-9653059-0

I dedicate this book with great love to my grandmother, Laura Phillips,
who always communicated with love

and

to Paula Rachel Kaufman, the embodiment of all that is Divine in my life.

I would like to extend heartfelt thanks to all of our Deva Family – your blessings are such an inspiration.

And to the following individuals who offered their spiritual, moral and financial support to me as I wrote this book:

Heide Birck	Don DeLaski
Ardis Burst	Ralfee Finn
Jo Dali	Werner Ruoff

With love forever ...

Rick

Contents

Letting Go

Winter has come with a wind of urgency,
communicating its yearly message once again.
The sun, low in the sky, is obscured
by the meaningful shadow of clouds;
the light of day wanders.

A young, delicate tree trembles
as the cold wind flows over and between
its barren branches.
Naked to the austerity of winter's touch,
the immaturity of its existence is tested.

Then for a moment, the clouds release their grip,
and the sun shines forth.
The tree invisibly turns toward the light,
and a single red leaf becomes visible;
it's shape that of a five-pointed star.

The light shines through,
illuminating the perfection of that single leaf.
Much has been lost—
all seeming to fall away.
The tree struggles with Winter's demand,
trying to hold onto its last identification with life.

But, with that moment of fleeting warmth,
the tree is reminded
that it is time to surrender.
That after rest,
growth will come once again.

Understanding,
now One with the Unity,
the tree becomes quiet,
and the wind withdraws
without a whisper.

In the stillness of Winter's moment,
the leaf falls to the ground,
and all of Nature celebrates.

PREFACE

The awareness of human separation—without reunion by love—is the source of shame. It is at the same time the source of guilt and anxiety.

Erich Fromm, *The Art of Loving*
(London: Unwin Books, 1962. Pg. 14)

At the autumn equinox of 1989, something shifted in my consciousness that would change my life forever. My wife, Paula Rachel Kaufman, and I were spending several weeks on the north shore of Kauai, Hawaii with some of our Deva Foundation* facilitators, enjoying the beauty of this blessed piece of paradise. We had just finished speaking with a dedicated environmentalist named Stan, a member of Earthtrust, regarding marine environmental issues so we could get updated on what had been happening and how Deva Foundation might be able to contribute. As a result, we were offered a Zodiac raft ride along the rugged Na Pali coast to search for dolphins. Earthtrust's boat only held 4 or 5 people so Rachel and I suggested that our facilitators take the trip since they would not have the opportunity again in the foreseeable future. (I must admit I was feeling a bit jealous because I really wanted to go.) The next day they set out and had a spectacular excursion but not a dolphin adventure; not one showed up to play.

A couple of days later, Stan called us and said that he had been thinking he would really like to take Rachel and me out

* Deva Foundation is a nonprofit educational and charitable U.S. organization which includes individual psychospiritual therapy. Deva Facilitators offer this type of healing work all over the world.

on the Zodiac because he knew we really wanted to go. Rachel immediately said, "Yes!" and it would be the perfect birthday present for me with my birthday only 2 days away. So on a beautiful Hawaii morning, we set out to enjoy the incredible wildness of Na Pali, and we kept our fingers crossed for dolphins. The round trip takes about two-and-a-half hours from Hanalei Bay, but after one-and-a-half hours we saw no dolphins anywhere. Moreover, the weather, which can change dramatically in a split second, was getting rough and dark quickly, so we started heading back. We were disappointed because dolphins are one of my favorite creatures, the incarnation of grace and the embodiment of all that is joyful in life. My only intimate moments with them were in the artificial showbiz environment of Sea World, which I had loved, but I had also felt the discomfort of their boundaries. On the other hand, I had felt that those dolphins and whales were giving an unconditional gift of themselves, to communicate their sentience to people.

All of a sudden we were in the middle of a storm. The waves seemed to be tossing us ten feet into the air, and the wind and rain sapped all the heat from my body. As I held on tightly in the bow of the raft, each wave drenched me to the point where I wanted to put my scuba mask on. I noticed that the current was quite vicious also because we were barely creeping along. After half an hour, it seemed that the weather was getting worse instead of better, and I wondered whether this was some kind of omen for my upcoming thirty-sixth year. I cringed at the thought. Then I looked back to see how Rachel was handling the excitement. She was holding onto the ropes with her eyes closed. I thought maybe she was terrified and was trying to pretend this wasn't happening; that she was actually horrified that we might drown. I continued to project my own fears of being ripped apart by sharks or becoming lost in the middle of the Pacific Ocean, dead of starvation and picked clean by seagulls. Obviously, my mind was as turbulent as the sea, but then I noticed Rachel's face was peaceful and quiet, as if she was in deep meditation, untouched by the storm (which later I found out was true). Within a few minutes the clouds had passed, the sun was out, and the sea was calming down. I sat there dumbfounded, asking myself if this was possible or whether it was some kind of miracle; although the real miracle was yet to come for within minutes we suddenly found ourselves surrounded by at least fifty dolphins. I let out a scream of disbelief and looked back at Rachel, who was just beaming. Stan gunned the Zodiac; playtime had arrived. The dolphins joyfully played with the waves and as if rehearsed, demonstrated their spinning leaps for us. Then I knew why these creatures were called Spinner Dolphins. There were at least two or three in the air at one time, putting on a show that would make Sea World look like child's play. I was ecstatic; I couldn't believe the intensity of the moment. As if they knew that I was ready to pass out from overload, they came up and splashed me to wake me up, to remind me that we were just having fun. Then a mother and her newborn baby swam up to the side (the baby couldn't have been more than 3 feet long). My heart exploded into tears; it was as if Mamma Dolphin wanted to introduce me to her baby, as if to say, "Isn't this child wonderful? Isn't life divine?"

I don't know how long we played with each other, but finally I found the courage to tell Stan that I wanted to go into the water with the dolphins. I knew his feelings about things like that: you don't interfere with the ecosystem, you don't hassle its creatures, in other words, you don't swim with the dolphins. I understood and even agreed, but I still wanted to be with them in their environment. A few minutes later I heard him say, "Well, OK, go on in." In a split second, I had my mask, snorkel and fins on, and was over the side.

Some moments are so exquisitely perfect that time stands

still and all desires fade into the crystal clarity of the moment. As I floated down beneath the surface, four dolphins swam up from the depths and turned on their sides to get a good look at me with that seemingly perpetual smile on their faces. Then I heard them. I heard with clarity the perfection of their call, like a whistle followed by clicking. But it wasn't the physical sound that put me into such a state of communion. Instantaneously, I was connected to their consciousness in a way that I had never known was possible. Their sound was like a mantra. It took me deep into myself, to a place that was comfortably familiar, a pure place of consciousness where I was one with the Dolphin-Self. Ours was a collective mind, a unified consciousness. It was in that moment I realized that the dolphins share a group awareness. Although each dolphin is an individual, there is no separation; there is only the knowing of oneness.

I felt that unified reality and I will never forget it. It is the same communal energy that makes a school of fish turn together instantly, as if a conductor were directing their concert, or a flock of birds that turn as one organism, one mind. The dolphins know no division; they bridge the expansiveness of the galactic into the third-dimension, spirit into matter, and in so doing they live their bliss in togetherness. They still hunt for fish and protect themselves from predators. Amazingly enough, they even forgive humanity's ignorance and insensitivity because they are unified, they are not separate from us. Because my mind was one with their consciousness, I knew that when the mother dolphin showed me her baby, she wanted to show me *our* baby. She trusted me and knew I would take care of her. And I knew that I would devote my life to her offspring, to do my best to educate the public about the environment through our educational and charitable work at Deva Foundation. More importantly, I would honor her by continuing to help people see our interconnectedness, to experience within ourselves that *we are not separate*, and to help find new ways to tear down the judgments that separate us from ourselves and each other. This book is that promise. Its purpose is to search deep into the energetic source of connectedness and the role that communication plays in our lives.

The dolphins have given me a great gift. Their unified consciousness made it painfully clear that I was a victim of separation, that my reality was governed by an aloneness that cut me off from life. It was so clear how addicted to separation we all are. How could a global society sanction the destruction of Mother Earth for the accumulation of material comforts, or ignore thousands of starving children, or repeat the pattern of war when history has recorded the suffering of such catastrophes? Only a deep-seated theme of separation obscures our view of the true reality of oneness, and the dolphins woke me up to this common illusion.

In a moment of ecstatic unity, my life moved onto another level, my path became more clear. The dolphins' gift of communication brought me an energy that opened my mind, that changed my reality, and that introduced me to the phenomenon of communion, that state of consciousness where only unity prevails in an expansive energetic connection.

As I integrated this experience, the dynamics of relationship became clearer. I realized that communication is the flow of energy that brings us into relationship. As consciousness expands by way of the heart, we start to come closer and closer until this intimate form of communication actually pulls us *into* each other. The gap between my-self and non-self disappears, and as the boundaries fall away, the true Self is revealed along with a state of unified connection I shall call *communion*. This book, then, is an inner and outer journey into the tangible and symbolic realm of communication as a fundamental path to communion.

Communication is not just reading, writing, and speaking. In its essence, it is the flow of energy and intelligence that connects the perceiver with the object of perception. This flow of energy, this communication, is truly multidimensional. It occurs on the level of the subatomic, and it occurs in the cells of our body. Any interaction in which energy is exchanged involves the process of communication. It is not limited to the voice, the printed page, or television, but includes the level of spirit and the multiple levels of human awareness. Communication is a basic function of creation, so profound that it becomes a path to union with God/dess. By becoming conscious about this fundamental principle, we can transform the dysfunctional aspects of our relationships to one another, to the world, and to God/dess.

When I returned home to New Mexico, my experiences with the dolphins synchronistically infused my clients' sessions with a new perspective about relationship. Every client I saw in the following months was saying, "I can't communicate with anybody anymore!" The blocks to experiencing unconditional love were, in essence, blocks to the ability to energetically connect through communication. My work at the Deva Foundation became the arena to investigate this fundamental process that lies at the core of relationship.

Since 1971, my investigation of the inner world has been the basis of my healing work with people. The Deva Session Work originally evolved out of my dedication to deep meditation as a spiritual path. It taught me how to go into the depths within myself and explore the spiritual landscapes. This is where pure potential lies waiting. Knowing this, I began taking people on the "grand exploratory tour."

In the last fifteen years, the value of assisting individuals into non-ordinary states of consciousness and watching the symbolic experiences arise, has repeatedly convinced me that everyone can connect to the power of Spirit. This Higher Self energy is omnipotent in its ability to heal and transform the attachments of karma held in our Emotional Body. As a facilitator of this beautiful process, I have watched my clients empower themselves with knowledge and open their hearts to the sacred.

My dedication to helping others clear their deepest karmic themes of separation/judgment had led me to the publication of my first book, *Emergence of the Divine Child*. I now realized that the next step would be to study and develop ways to become more conscious of communication as a path to unity. So after several years of being taught by my clients and students, plus a lot of inner work, I tackled the most challenging and exciting project of my life.

This book investigates finding the path to unity by becoming conscious of one of humanity's truly great challenges: communication. Our ability to communicate is inhibited by our feelings of detachment, aloneness, disconnection—in other words, the theme of separation.

The overshadowing power of separation is almost unimaginable. It is as dense an energy as any, and it is the ultimate delusion because it seems *normal*. So we live it, reinforce it, and depend upon it to validate our world of suffering as we uphold our continual withdrawal from the truth that *life is unified consciousness*. To fathom the existence of separation is a major realization because it opens a window of opportunity to its complement, the power of unity.

To play within unity is to flirt with a fresh approach to life, including new, expansive rules and attitudes, and radically different experiences of our relationships, our work, and our purpose. It affects the simplest of behaviors—for example, instead of seeing a tree, I merge with the tree so that there is no subject and no object, only oneness. Instead of tasting the apple, I am the sweetness of the apple. In relationships, I am united with the essence of the other. The degree of unity may vary as may the degree of separation, yet something within us knows this state of reality. Then we can consciously allow it to unfold and to be expressed as our habitual behaviors of entrapped routines release their age-old grip. What once seemed impossible dawns as the creative juice of transformation and rebirth.

New realities are a great relief and a healing potion to a heart that has become sick of the prisons of discontent. The true nature of the heart is unbounded, unconditional, and bravely accepting of relationship as the spirited dance of Unity. The communion of the heart is not just a state of loving kindness; it is the tangible reality of God/dess consciousness grounded in human life. My dolphin experience set into motion an extraordinary personal unfoldment that has culminated in the writing of this book at this important time in our collective unfoldment.

1

Listening to the Higher Self

The truths of human life tend to be hidden. Enshrouded in the webs of illusion, we get caught in the "game" until we are playing so intensely that our primary intention has been forgotten. Trapped by the marvels of perception on the human plane, we are drawn outward through the senses into the phenomenal world and the attachments of karma, emotion, and the mysteries of life. Yet there is a firm foundation of reality within us, at times beyond our conscious perception, yet nevertheless constantly there as our true reality. This divine source is eternal, conscious, and equally available to everyone. It is the Higher Self, the self that exists beyond the confines of the incarnational games and roles we play. This Higher Self can guide us, teach us, and certainly thrill us, for it truly is our one and only spiritual source, our connection to the Divine Imagination. To investigate its ways of communication and to open to the flow of conscious spiritual insight is an inspired purpose for our lives. Its potential is utterly profound.

At the Deva Foundation, our psychospiritual facilitators help people open the doors to their spiritual truths, facilitating the clearing of emotional patterns of illusion and unconsciousness. Spiritual energy is indeed the greatest healer, the Higher Self being the teacher and guide for the mastery of life. To expand our consciousness of this unlimited source within, we must begin by learning the language of our inner spiritual world and becoming skilled in the exploration of its multidimensional landscape.

One of the amazing benefits of being a Deva Facilitator is to watch a client's Higher Self ingeniously manifest experiences to heal the karmic issues of life. It is truly miraculous to see inner knowing flow into problems, or clarify a state of denial or confusion, or to see spiritual energy transform our attachments of who we think we are.

The creative expressions of consciousness that are seen in psychospiritual sessions, meditation, or dreams are rich in symbolism. Always multidimensional, these inner experiences affect our sense of reality *holographically* and provide our intellect with marvelous understandings. To have the privilege of watching and sharing in a client's mystical journey is a great opportunity. Not only is the information always relevant, but the power of a spiritual question and the penetration into deeper and deeper levels of understanding ushers in new possibilities, allowing both the facilitator and the client to creatively communicate with new models of reality as the sense of Self evolves.

The following part of a session with Samantha is unique in that. Instead of processing issues for the purpose of releasing emotional attachment, the Higher Self channels a lucid understanding of the nature of Self. This experience is coming from that aspect of Higher Self that we may call *higher mind,* which has the effect of clearing clouds of ignorance and misunderstanding.

A Session with Samantha

Samantha: *I keep hearing the question, "Who am I?" I'm not sure who or what the "I" is....*

I ponder and create an answer, I construct a "description" of who—the words are interesting: ponder, create, construct—*I am a white female; blonde and blue-eyed, five feet, nine inches tall, who does this and that, and who believes such and such. But if I have lived in another body before; the physical description was different, the activities I have done were different, my beliefs were based on another time and another culture, the events of my life were different, and therefore the lessons of life were different. I was a different being....*

Then I draw the conclusion that "who I am" is a spirit that inhabits different bodies, does different things, believes different ideas, and so on. But the spirit is not the body. It doesn't do anything, including ponder ideas or fight for beliefs; it is just the silent witness who observes the relative world of manifestation from a place of silent, unmanifest, pure being. The silence is the only thing that feels real. The rest of it just seems part of a grand, unfathomable game.

I prefer the expansiveness of the silence....

Now I hear the question, "Why am I here?" I construct an answer based on purpose, activity to fulfill that purpose, and so on, yet the answer assumes that I (something incarnate) am here (... a locus in time and space that exists); therefore, if I exist in the relative world (which only the model in the mind assumes), then I can construct reasons for doing that. If I don't exist here, because all this is just a thoughtform, there is nothing to do, nowhere to go, no purpose to accomplish, no "why" to answer, no "here" to be in. There is just pure being, and here I am again!...

Regardless of my answers, which are based on my perceptions, beliefs, understanding, and my ability to communicate, ideas are only constructs of my mind—a model of the so-called reality that I have conjured up.

It's ironic that we talk about sentient beings as those that are conscious that they exist, aware of their awareness. And *yet to be aware that I exist is a type of illusion, because this form does not **truly** exist. We say that the tree is not aware that it exists, as well as the turtle, the mosquito, and so on. We are aware they exist, but they are not aware. Does that mean I have created the existence of these forms as part of my reality? How could they create themselves without awareness? If they have a spirit that is one with God, how do they realize that? Does that soul evolve to higher and higher realms of consciousness to reach the point where it realizes it was all illusion? Then does it let go of the boundaries, to be merged into the Absolute Oneness?*

How do we let go of the illusion? What is it that chooses to let go?

I hear the word surrender, but it is not a choice, it is a process that creeps up on you in the night and slowly dissolves the need to hold on. Yes, that's it—so clear. It's another state of mind that allows the model of who I think I am to be dissolved into just being what is—the ability to be here, now, with no need to identify with the act of the doer.

Illusion exists as long as I maintain a context or model for what I, the observer, observe as the object of perception, or as long as the subject identifies with the object of perception.

Identification is the act of losing oneself in the object of perception. When the subject dissolves or is overshadowed and only the object remains, a false or illusory unity of consciousness exists, for example.

It's so amazing how these experiences become so clear, so simple.

When I feel angry or when I watch a film or read a book, instead of experiencing self-consciousness, I experience the anger, the drama of the film or the book, where I forget myself in the experience. We commonly hear, "I didn't realize I ate the whole box of popcorn—that movie was really absorbing," or "I don't know why I got angry, I just lost myself in it; but

I'm better now, and I'm sorry." The more we lose ourselves in the experience of some event, the more power the experience has over us and the more we lose our sense of being....

Now I understand. I feel totally in tune, a communication of such clarity; my Higher Self is certainly the greatest of all gurus.

(End of session)

Models of Reality

Living in a body demands that we live in a world of matter and energy. This produces forms, and we identify with those forms. How we understand our perceptions of the things around us requires us to reorganize our sensory input so that we can recognize a perception and be able to interact or communicate with it. In order to do this, we create models of reality.

These models can include habitual behavioral responses, learned from parents and society. We are taught how to live, how to react, what is right or wrong. We form attitudes based on our programming from the past. We are taught how to relate, what to believe, and even what we are supposed to be. Models can be symbolic or representational forms that create a lens for us to view manifest reality.

We create the "model airplane" to represent something tangible, or we "model behavior" of the judge, honor student, athlete, etc., or enjoy watching a "fashion model" display the elegance or "look" that we consider ideal. Underneath all this imprinting and programming is an emotional body that just *feels*. It holds a set of emotional responses that are based on its programming since its creation, countless lifetimes ago. Since the emotional body exists outside of time and space, its imprinting makes it vulnerable at any moment to repeat the responses of the past, including pre-incarnational memory, here in the present. When it does get triggered, its emotional energy associates itself with the events and situations of the moment, creating another memory layer which then attaches to the seed memory of the past. Each layer strengthens our emotional identification with the memories of the past by trapping us in the models of limitation and suffering.

Our mental judgments and attitudes then reflect these emotional imprints, and we constantly express them in our daily behavior. The karmic imprints held in the emotional body, therefore, are the basis of how we see and act in the world. Our karma has created our models of reality. The greater the attachment to these karmic models, the less consciousness we will experience. Or we can say that the more we identify with the emotional imprints of the past, the less conscious we will be of the unbounded nature of Spirit and the sense of freedom it holds.

To transcend models is to go beyond manifestation into a merging with the Absolute Oneness. Then, of course, there is no body, no incarnational need. But we *are* in body and we are in need of further growth. *How do we live in a body, realize the ultimate, and live enlightenment in a world of form?*

The first step requires us to experience something besides the relative world of form. We must know the experience of the Absolute Oneness, which by definition is formless and unmanifest. Until we have experienced the source of all matter and energy that structures form, we are unable to live the coexistence of the absolute and relative worlds.

For example, we may have two glasses of clear water. They may look alike, but until we use another way of perceiving—such as taste—we miss the experience of the dissolved salt in one and the dissolved sugar in another. Relying on singular means of perception, we cannot distinguish the false assumptions we've made and cannot move beyond the illusion of the familiar experience.

In order to experience the formless, we must take our attention inward, into the silence of pure consciousness, that absolute field of being. Meditation is one method that is direct and a natural way to experience the unmanifest world from which all form arises.

The second step is to become aware of our models of reality, which include both mental and emotional imprints of the past. The overshadowing effect of our memory causes us to lose sight of our unbounded nature, and this leads to suffering. If the Buddha is correct that one cause of suffering is ignorance, then the influence of memory has caused us to fall into the trap of "ignoring" our essential nature, which is beyond the constraint of the thoughtforms of memory.

Pure knowledge of the true nature of Self is enough to loosen the grip of ignorance which has perpetuated attachment to the models and concepts of who and what we think we are. This knowledge is not of the mind, but of the Higher Self. We may also call it the intuitive heart, or the Divine Heart. It is known by the totality of who I am—Spirit. The mind is trapped in its models; the intuitive heart can let go of models, and in its expansiveness can feel truth without needing to explain or put it into form. The essence of who we truly are knows itself; coming back to an experience of that essence allows it to integrate into our incarnate life.

To become conscious of our models of reality also means to recognize that we create models, and models require structures of matter and energy. Whether it be a model of "good" behavior, or a model of our planet in a universe of celestial objects, these models are creations and therefore move through their cycles of change. They are the "stuff" of the relative world, as "real" as any other manifestation of creation. Yet they are real only from the perspective of the relative world. To know the Absolute Oneness is to be looking from a unique and different viewpoint. As a result, our perception of relative reality has changed. Absolute Oneness is now what is "real," and the relative world has the feel of the illusory. Because our manifest world is constantly changing, moving through the cycles of creation and dissolution, only Absolute Oneness has the *unchanging stability* of eternity and the intelligence to uphold the template of creation.

If there is a goal, it would be to realize Absolute Oneness as the source and all models of form as temporary and illusory. To only identify with the relative world leads to ignorance, which leads to suffering. That is what we have done. Recognizing Absolute Oneness brings us back home to what is truly our reality.

The third step, which is a natural progression of our expanding consciousness, is to clear the attachments of the emotional body and infuse knowledge of Spirit into our daily life. As this progresses, our happiness and success in living naturally spills out to our world and, by our example, others are positively affected. The realization of God/dess spreads through the collective consciousness.

Form is created by karma. The spirit infuses form. The spirit is not the karma, and therefore not the form, but coexists with it. Spirit is transcendental, beyond form and structure. Our models of reality are created from the influence of karma and our identification or attachment to it.

Our Higher Self, in its pure formlessness, is unbounded and not localized in time and space because it is omnipresent, multidimensional, and transcendental. Yet we symbolically give it form and meaning as we strive to know it and come into integration with it. We require the formless to assume a form so that the initial steps of communication can give us a sense of contact and inspiration—an infusion within the mind and body of the reality of the spiritual.

Because of our limitations, we model our communication behavior after our interpersonal relationships. We need to hear, touch, see, and feel the reactions within others and, in the same way, we require the same intimacy from our Higher Self.

One reason that channeling has become popular is that the invisible entity talks with us from beyond, modeling a telephone call. Speech is the model of behavior that links us to a spiritual entity in another realm. The entity adapts to our sensory needs of experience. The Higher Self may do the same; as a result, we have a tendency to want to precipitate it into form, into a model that is easy to experience and that conforms to our ideas of what it is supposed to be.

The more we live in our left-brain, linear views of life, the greater need we have to experience the Higher Self as a tangible form that we can experience with our five senses. From those senses, we usually require the Higher Self to be somewhat like us, with a personality that we respect, preferably quite holy and wise. This personality is our ego's need. The Higher Self's symbolic form is not real but is a model that we have created to make it easier for us to relate to our True Self. The symbolism of the form and the behavior we perceive are just the creation we require as we move down the path of evolution. As consciousness expands and our linear perspectives fall away, our need for a three-dimensional personal form gives way to a more abstract form. Our model has expanded.

So what we see happening is a progression of models. Each successive form becomes a little more open and a little more expansive, with greater compassion, greater freedom, and greater unconditional love, until the model is so expansive that all the boundaries fall away and we are left with a conception of Self that is unlimited and transcendental. In other words, we are left with *no model at all*, nothing with which to identify. We are within the infinity of it all. We come into unity consciousness of everlasting being.

As You Believe: God Consciousness in Action

In 1976, I was teaching a meditation class in which one of my students, a ten-year-old boy named Scott, had just finished playing in a junior golf tournament. He was quite interested in meditation because his parents had been meditating for several years. One day he said he wanted to learn to meditate too, so they suggested he give me a call. I asked him why he wanted to learn, and he said there were three reasons: he had read that athletes meditate so that they can play sports better; his parents were nicer to him since they started meditating; and his mom said that when you meditate, it's like being part of God, and that feels good. Also, he said he had been going to Sunday school at his church, and for the last few weeks they had been talking about God and how God created the world, the animals, and all that "stuff." It made him feel good that God could create things and do whatever He wanted without someone telling Him what to do.

I realized this kid was really jazzed up. I quickly told him I'd be glad to teach him and we started the following week. After four days of instruction, on the last evening of our meditation class, Scott told us quite a story about a golf tournament he was currently playing in. He was on the last hole of his nine-hole course and playing pretty well. He had to wait a few minutes before he teed-off; it was a short par three, and the kids in front were having a lot of trouble, so his foursome had to wait until the others were off the green. While he was waiting, he was thinking about his meditation and about God creating the world. He thought, "If I meditate and can become part of God, then maybe I can create whatever I want." He said it made perfect sense to him.

He stepped up to the tee and pulled out his four-wood. As he prepared to hit the ball, he felt a wave of warmth come through his body and a feeling of strength, which he noticed because up until then he had felt very tired. Then he said that he felt like God. When I asked what that felt like, he simply said, "It felt like I could do anything!" I was in awe listening to this boy because I could see some of that radiance coming through him while he was talking.

"Then I started my swing," he said. "It was like you see on TV when they do those slow-motion replays, and when I hit the ball, I knew it was going in. It was beautiful. The ball hit in front of the green, bounced twice, hit the pin, and dropped straight down into the hole. And boy, did I scream!" Scott was just radiating bliss. "I knew that I was part of God and, you know, God can make a hole-in-one!"

From his boyish innocence, Scott manifested a simple fulfillment of his desire. It all made sense to him; he believed and it was proven true. In his consciousness he believed that he could become part of God and that God can create anything. That God-part within Scott created an experience that is the dream of any golfer. Ninety-eight percent of all golfers go through their entire lives without shooting a hole-in-one. If we are one with God, a hole in one is not hard to do. What we believe is what we are. If we are identified with limitations, then they become our reality. If we transcend the illusions and expand into the possibility of God, then God becomes real and life changes.

Throughout history, the concept of God has been overlaid by human projections. God is a father, God is a mother, God is a punishing force, God fights with Satan, God only forgives those who repent, my God is better than your God, and on and on. These projections illustrate the limits and the programming of people in any given time and culture. We lock onto the one who has performed a miracle and suppose that he or she must be a knower of God and a prophet. We look to others to teach us about God, or we select one scripture above all others to be our testament of truth. With this approach, God will always be relative to our particular point of view. God will be different to me than to you. We will understand the concept somewhat differently until we experience communion. Then, and only then, will the observer and the observed (in this case the experience of God) merge into oneness, where I am God, God is me, and we are one. As soon as we exit that experience, we are back in the relative world and our words no longer adequately describe that reality; but inside there is an imprinting of the truth that is always known. The reality of God consciousness becomes permanent, twenty-four hours a day, only when communion is the steadfast basis of all experience. We start with the precious moment of communion and we keep inviting it back until it never fades away.

Connection to Spirit, Letting Go of Separation

Eventually we will realize our true Self. Enlightenment will dawn and ignorance will disappear as if we had awakened from a long night's sleep. The gap between the ego's concept of self and the Higher Self will be dissolved into the unity of Self, but until that time, it is important to open the communication channel between the ego and our deepest essence.

The following two sessions are mine. I was reluctant at first to use these sessions in this book, especially under my name, but I realized that these experiences have a commonality with those of many people at this time, and that I need to boldly speak my truth, which is what I want this book to express. These are my issues and these are touching universal themes, one of which is the theme of separation.

My Higher Self needed to bring to my consciousness the memories and examples of separation in order to then open my ability to communicate, both inwardly to the Higher Self or outwardly to life.

Session 1

Rick: *I don't feel much, especially in my heart....*

Facilitator: Just be in that. See what happens.

Rick: *My stomach feels like it is distended, as if I were pregnant. I'm getting the sense of memories of pregnancies, subtle feelings of more than one lifetime of traumatic pregnancy. I feel myself as female and I'm having a very difficult time with this pregnancy. I'm unable to give birth, unable to deliver the baby. There's a blockage or something preventing the baby from coming out....*

Now I realize that this is a very familiar memory; it must have happened many times in many lifetimes. I die trying to give birth. I feel this as both mother and child. As the mother I feel the pain, the sense of incredible loss, such devastation of loss. I feel there's no way to save the baby, no way to tell the baby what's happening....

As the baby, I sense the struggle around me. I feel Mother separating; I'm losing her. In losing her I lose my sense of self. I'm pulled back into the void....

Now I feel the familiar memory of my birth in this present lifetime. I was six weeks premature, so in this hospital they took me from Mother and put me into an incubator. Such aloneness! I'm totally isolated with no human contact, just left in this sterile, artificial environment, all alone. There's no touch, no love, no connection with anything or anyone. I feel aloneness as nothingness, as no feeling. This lack of stimulation and contact is in conflict with the needs of the child for Mother, but he is not being fulfilled. I feel this contradiction. The imprint creates a feeling that alone is normal, but this can only happen when my needs and feelings are repressed or shutdown. My needs for connection, for nourishment are numbed out, but they still exist in an unfulfilled place within me. I see how that feeling today prevents me from really letting go. I've created a barrier of protection and control, and it won't let me transcend.

It's a funny thing that I can't go deeper into that feeling. I stay in my analytical mind so I can watch it from a distance. My mind tells me of all these issues and their connection to my life. Why can't I let myself feel? It's the pattern. I live this contradiction between perpetually feeling aloneness and the need to not feel alone. It's a vicious cycle with no break in it....

Facilitator: Feel yourself as the child. What's happening?

Rick: *I look to see if this child is crying, and as I expected, he is not....*

Now I see myself at about four years old. It's nighttime, and I feel anxiety. My parents aren't there. I feel such abandonment. I'm manic, running around full of distress, just aloneness in my abandonment. I'm needing them, and they aren't there, such uncontrollable anxiety.

I see the baby in the incubator. It's so sad...(Pause)

My Higher Self appears as the Divine Child, radiant, full of feeling. Its energy is so Divine, so light. He comes and touches the left side of my head, the temporal lobe. He says my speech center holds all these memories, like a genetic flaw. It has prevented me from giving voice to my feelings, from being able to communicate, to connect energetically on the inside and outwardly to the world, especially to people. The aloneness, the abandonment, the separation has held me literally speechless, trapped in the void of separation, alone with the karmic reality of aloneness...(Tears)

I feel there's no escape. I either feel the desolation of the aloneness or I shut it down into no feeling at all. Or I create a drama-especially in relationships, where I trigger an intense emotional reaction which usually ends up in pain for myself and others. Then I separate and shut it down again, and the process repeats over and over.

There's a reluctance to go deeper into these feelings; the pain of the aloneness is too much, I'm afraid to feel it again, to feel the void....

The aloneness seems to be as close as you can get to "no ego," a feeling of being completely dissolved, fragmented into nothingness. It's the same as having no mother. It's a gap in my male-female connection. My masculine energy jumps in there with control and the ability to be strong, to let the power of the mind body be dominant. The feminine is almost nonexistent; it never was created. Mother never bonded. There is such a need for the feminine energy to emerge, to connect and to nourish me, but the masculine grip is strong in its protective function. It won't let go, as if it doesn't trust the feminine to be available. It wasn't there before; why should it be there now?

I've always craved for the breast; I was never breast-fed. In this life there has been a strong urge to connect sexually as a way to connect to someone, to find Mother, but Mother obscures woman. Women want to be equal in partnership, to have a merging of yin and yang, not to just be a mother surrogate.

It's such a jumbled mess. There's such an imprint of confusion. What's normal? All these themes are so habituated, grooved into a way of being. There's nothing but this model of reality I can manifest. It's also the unfortunate reality of the world. How do we learn to connect? To experience bonding? What does it really mean to be one with another person? I have preferred to space-out into galactic experience where feelings are different, where there's no pain, just expansiveness. Where the mind can be stimulated, interested, and lost in its games of perception and change. But with human relationships, it's a different game. I find it more difficult and it's certainly more painful. I'm caught in separation/judgment issues as a way to perpetuate my separation from people and Self.

I find it amazing. All this stuff is falling into place. The picture is clearer. On some level, I've known much of this, but it was never integrated before. The symbol of my separation at birth pulls it all together for this lifetime....

I feel a strong vibration in my body; it undulates from my feet up to my head. I feel very open. I realize that seeing the pieces fall together is the change. The feelings aren't powerful, but I feel a shift. It's like experiencing aloneness from another level, yet the attachment is gone. There's just a desire to clear all this out. I ask for guidance and I see my Divine Child there smiling, as if there's not a concern in the world.

I feel pretty complete now; I just want to rest with it.
(End of session)

Session 2

Rick: *There is a desire to experience a state beyond ego identification, but I realize that any experience that I would speak out would be an identification. I feel the predicament....*

I want to go beyond it all and I want to express it, but every time I start to speak it out, the energy changes, there's a disruption.

Now I shift my focus and I see how it's possible to

experience without the sensory apparatus, to perceive without the senses. I move beyond the physical body into where there are no eyes, no ears, no senses at all, just mind. It has the ability to sense from a deeper area, just like a person who was born blind but who can still see. I go deeper....

It's so hard to find the appropriate words. In this state of consciousness beyond the senses, there is the ability to cognize, to realize that it has nothing to do with the senses. We don't get to practice that much because we are constantly caught in the outer direction of the bodily senses; we rely on them completely. If the senses are gone or turned off, then there is a natural state of knowing.

There is some curiosity or desire to "know." It happens due to ego-identification. The situation of the subject and the object of perception require some degree of identification or some overshadowing effect from the experience. If you take the object away, then you are left with the observer, but if you take the observer away, there can be no experience. If you take the ego away from the observer, then the object of perception cannot overshadow; there is nothing to bind or attach to because the observer is just consciousness itself, unbounded and nonlocal. Communication is only necessary when there is an ego that needs to bridge the gap of separation into a connection with something that is perceived as other than itself. The ego strives to connect that which is not connected, to create a unity. The ego exists in a state that is disconnected and separate. It gets overshadowed because this self-identity views itself as something distinct and different from everything else.... So I have to go beyond the ego to bridge separation.

Communication begins the process by connecting that which I have perceived as separate. It energetically links the ego to the observed, even if the observed is pure consciousness. But when the ego experiences that which has no bound-

aries, no definition, no-thing to identify with, then it begins to merge. In the merging begins the dissolution of the boundaries of the ego. Everything it thought it was has to fall away. It resists at first, because it believes it will die, it will cease to exist. This is true, but consciousness remains—that very same consciousness that is the essence of all manifest creation, our absolute nature.

My mind is blowing my mind. Or I should say Higher Mind is blowing my ego mind?...

How is it possible that a person can be free of ego and yet still be in a body that experiences the outer world? How could there be a sense of self?

Facilitator: Ask your Higher Self.

Rick: *I see myself floating on an infinite ocean. On the surface of the ocean there is a small ripple. But whether you look from high above or from the surface level, there is just flat infinite ocean vibrating below. On one small spot on the ocean is an area that is free of motion; it looks like glass. All around it the ripple agitation can be seen. But this glassy place is different, though it is ocean also. I am that flat glassy spot.*

A bird in the sky flies over me and for a moment the bird reflects off of my surface. The bird at that instant has connected to me, the energy of reflection has joined us together—I am the bird and I am the ocean. Then the bird is gone and now I reflect the sun; and, for some time, I am the sun too. While I reflect the sun I also feel heat, warmth. I am so much. I truly am multidimensional. Then I reflect the sky.

The glassy part disappears as the rippling wave spreads over the surface. I am the ocean, indistinguishable from it now.

Whether I am the bird or the sun or the heat or the sky, my main awareness is that of the ocean. These other experiences were transitory. Only the constancy of the ocean is eternal. The flow of change comes and goes and I, as the ocean, can experience that flow, but I don't lose my awareness of Self in the experience.

I am the infinite, absolute, uniform ocean, but I can still precipitate into form as the bird or sun. That form has boundaries and characteristics, but it is just the reflection, an illusion that is transitory. It will disappear and I will come back to my true reality....

Communication is only relevant from the perspective of the relative world looking toward the infinite. Communication is a striving of form to experience the formless, the unbounded. But once the experience has merged into infinity, there is no need to communicate; there is just communion. The drop of water realizes it is the ocean. There is no need to connect to the ocean when I realize it is already me.

In relation to the ego, once the dissolution of the ego is experienced permanently, it makes no difference if I take form or not. Only the avatar takes form. Symbolically, the avatar comes into form to initiate the Way, to catalyze change or, in personal terms, to help and serve by modeling enlightenment. In a sense, the only conscious manifestation of Absolute Oneness is the avatar; everything else is holding some identification with form.

My mind gets so confused with this....

Facilitator: Let go of mind and move back into pure cognition.

Rick: *It just seems to be a matter of degree. The avatar symbolizes the highest category of conscious form and intention, yet there must be a gradation of lesser categories. If I had two enlightened people in front of me with the same realization of the Infinite, they would still appear to be two different people with various talents and tendencies. On the*

*level of the superficial, they are different; on the level of
Absolute they are one. Depending on my perspective, I discern
a greater or lesser grade, but from their perspective, it is
absurd and meaningless.*

*Why do I care? Why does my mind indulge in this form of
spiritual materialism?...*

*All I can say is that my mind wants to stretch, to reach for
the infinite. It will expand as far as it will go, and then it will
have to let go. It needs to understand, to find meaning in the
chaos, order in an insane world of illusion. It needs to know
the truth. Even with everything else in process, it desires to see
the perfection of each step.*

*I'm familiar with looking at the formless from the
perspective of the ego/form, but I always retreat into form. I
can feel how the resonance of the formless, since it is
omnipresent, can be perpetuated, but the ego requires
constructs of form to be used as a point of reference, allowing
the experience to be distinguished on the level of mind, and the
energy to be felt and integrated on the level of the emotional
body....*

*There's something missing; I can't quite expand enough
to get it. I feel that familiar frustration. How do I hold the
reality of the formless while in the body? I come back to this....*

*My Higher Self keeps repeating the word grace. I'm not
sure I fully understand the significance of that word.*

Facilitator: Go into the energy of that word; go into grace.

Rick: *Yes! Of course!...*

You just know. *You just are that; there's no gap. You
always know that. It's not a matter of being told; it's not a
matter of mind. It's a state of cognition into a state of being.
Words are so inadequate, yet I got it. It's the realization that
you are touched with the "grace of knowing" until that*

knowing of the unboundedness is so normal, a component of all experience that is unshakably penetrated into the fabric of my reality. It bridges the gap into a unified experience. This process is not a matter of doing anything, but the experience of knowing is beyond the realm of form. It makes so much sense now. It's a dawning into enlightenment, where there is a bridging of the gap between the world of form and the formless until that instant when you just know, which is different from the feeling of a transitory taste. That experience of pure knowledge dissolves all ignorance of the past, present, and future, and you're left with an experience that never fades because you are now beyond time and space. It's so incredible!

I feel the taste of it, as if it was a soft intuitive touch. It moves through my mind as a gentle breeze, opening new pathways of consciousness. There's a sense of freshness, a hovering presence above and behind me.

There are no words to describe this, but I feel it as infinitely solid, stable in its unchangability. There's a sense of its ultimate groundedness. Change has no effect when you have that feeling. Change cannot overshadow it. It is the ultimate sanctuary, being at home, at rest, the absolute extinguishing of any desire to desire. There is no need to ever leave that place or do anything. There is no need of activity, no need to incarnate into form, just simply no need!

So why would an avatar come out of that place? Why would there be any desire to go into the world of form? Or be interested in the dramas of the dimensional worlds? It seems so far away and meaningless. Yet the manifest world is not separate from the unmanifest reality. So if it's not separate, then the suffering world sends some ripple through the ocean. And whereas the formless is beyond suffering, God must be touched by the suffering or any other feeling. The unmanifest senses it.

I remember the gap and that subtlest state of feeling.

There I remember that powerful sense of love and compassion. On that platform of duality, love creates its opposite, compassion creates its opposite. The condition of the opposites, love and hate—or rather love and separation, compassion and its opposite, the wish for suffering—this all moves in cycles. It is a flow of attachment and liberation, aggression and compassion. So by realizing that instead of identifying with the dramas of the cycle, you can just be in the process of helping—or rather, you become the "helping." Instead of getting stuck in the freeze-frame of time, you are that part of God that is the flow—a verb, like "Godding." That's it! "Godding!"

Now I can just melt, no more need for words.

(End of session)

These two sessions are interesting for many reasons. The first session is classic in that it brings together the karmic theme of separation (repeated through lifetimes) and my current life memory of separation from my mother at birth. Both are symbolic, regardless of whether they are "real" or not. What *is* real is the emotional body's attachment to the reoccurring separation theme and the problems with intimacy. The dynamics of shutting down the emotions, coupled with the inability to connect or communicate, is a common mode for us in our attempts to defend ourselves against pain.

The expansion of consciousness provided in the session allowed me to clear the clouds of confusion and unknowingness which are symptoms that have blocked my healing. The clearing occurs energetically because *the experience is the clearing*. The shifting of perspective into an expanded viewpoint allows the Higher Self to manifest as the Divine Child who, being free and available, "substitutes" for the *wounded* child with his spiritual presence. The Higher Self provides the healing of the past and brings the present into completion.

The healing of the separation theme of the second session permits me to go boldly into the "nothingness." Now that the fear of separation is released, there is a willingness to step beyond the ego. This session is unusual in that Higher Mind is producing exquisite cognitions of the predicament of the ego reality and its structure in space/time. Local Mind is dissolved in the expansiveness of Higher Mind, that free flow of creativity and intelligence.

As I said, "My mind is blowing my mind." I sense ego awareness disappearing in the presence of my Higher Self discourse. Anyone who witnessed this session would have also seen the quickening of vibration in my physical body which was so obviously powerful in the room. My Higher Self was channeling and the remnants of the ego allowed questions and issues to surface so the Higher Self could then deliver understanding—not just on an intellectual level but multidimensionally, even at a cellular level. Again, due to the expansion of consciousness in the session, the experience was the clearing and as a result I was transformed through it.

These sacred moments of communication with the Absolute transform us and illustrate, without a doubt, the power of the divine within all of us. They open the chakras. They align and balance the communication process so that afterwards, new pathways are activated and a new means of inner and outer dialogue becomes available to us in everyday life. We are listening to our Self.

2

Listening to Ourselves

Listening to ourselves is more than just listening to our thoughts and observing our feelings; it is an art. The ability to listen and perceive with expanded consciousness is something we learn, a skill we can refine. It depends on our willingness to slow down and pay attention. This is a fundamental principle of effective communication behavior.

In our session work at the Deva Foundation, the client develops the skill of listening to his or her self. As we move inside ourself, consciousness expands, thereby showing us what we need to see or hear. The experience consists of what the Higher Self needs to communicate to the conscious mind, whether it wants to open blocked or repressed feelings or experience old karmic themes such as anger, fear, or sadness. We are shifting awareness away from the outer, externalized means of knowing ourselves. Our awareness, usually based on social programming and our relative models, shifts. The mirroring that takes place in external relationships continually affirms our ego's need to have a visible sense of self that is based on those models of who we think we are. As we shift our viewpoint inwardly and peel away the layers of ego identification, what we experience is an emerging encounter with our Universal Self. Its nature is of infinite silence. What we experience as our essence is not based on doing, but simply being at one with the whole. *To listen to the Higher Self is to hear the eternal silence.* When this ultimate level is integrated into our consciousness, all other dimensions of self are also integrated and resonate together in perfect synchrony; the messages from our essential being are perceived powerfully, devoid of noise or confusion. Communication with our Higher Self is effortless and natural.

Separation/Judgment and the Throat Chakra

Communication begins with consciousness. The next step is the intention to bring that consciousness into relationship, whether it be with others or ourself. In order to tune into our personal self, we must be reasonably aware of the structure and function of our physical body, our feelings, and our expressions and behaviors. Ultimately, we transcend the forms and experience pure consciousness, the true nature of Self.

Consciousness, the view-screen of the mind, may be obscured by a physical limitation or by the effect of our emotional state of being. Since the emotional body colors our ability to perceive, like looking through colored sunglasses where everything we see is tinted by the color, the limiting karma of the emotional body negatively affects communication. Specifically, the primordial energy of separation is the fundamental bias that creates the themes of judgment, which then perpetuates separation.

In other words, instead of separation being our reality which influences our perception and identity, we are able to see through it as the illusion that it is.

Being able to focus our consciousness on ourself in order to listen to what is happening in our inner world is a process of going deeper and deeper, peeling the onion of karmic illusion, until the *veils of separation* become transparent. This inward path takes us into the realm of energy, into the subtle levels of our being.

When the throat chakra is inhibited, its coordinating and

synthesizing function is diminished. Mind, body, and emotions are unable to integrate and open to experience Spirit. In other words, these aspects are held in a constricted, low vibratory state. As a result, we communicate only on a superficial level, unable to communicate deeply both with ourselves and others. Our communicative energy just doesn't have the penetrative force that it could. It is like the difference between a forty-watt light bulb and a laser beam: one is diffuse and has a very limited range; the other is coherent and powerful and can span vast distances, piercing through the superficial. When our emotional body holds onto powerful themes like separation/judgment, our ability to communicate is severely limited. Unable to truly connect with others, we live isolated lives as victims of separation. Believing that we are alone and insignificant, our ego affirms our limited reality; and that perspective results in the loss of ourselves rather than our experiencing the unity of relationship.

Physical Body

We human beings are created with innumerable "feedback loops" that bring information back into our various systems in order to maintain physiological homeostasis. A simple feedback loop can be characterized by the body's need for temperature regulation. If our temperature drops, then circulation is adjusted and the skin changes in order to diminish heat loss. If we are too hot, our body changes to promote sweating, which relieves us of excess heat. Our internal thermostat works automatically without the need for conscious thought. The flow of sensation within the body's feedback loops is constantly adjusting, correcting, and balancing our internal environment.

We have taken this process of listening to our physical

body a step further in Western medicine with the creation of countless tests in order to understand the functioning of the body. To aid the body's ability to heal itself, the doctor first determines what the problem is through tests and diagnosis and then takes corrective action. Although science has excelled in this task, it has not taken us very far in our ability to listen to our body as it tries to tell us what is happening inside, either physically or emotionally. Our educational system spends little time helping us understand the cycles and messages of our physical body, not to mention those of our emotional body.

As with any form of communication, consciousness is the key to listening to ourselves. Learning to be aware is an important step in communicating with our various dimensions of being.

Traditional systems of medicine can teach us many effective techniques of mind/body perception and time-tested philosophies to help us interpret the information. Through my studies of Chinese medicine and Ayurveda, the ancient medicine of India, it has become clear that in order for medicine to be truly effective it must deal with all dimensions of life. Western medicine may be advanced in certain areas, like surgery, but it has not achieved an advanced level of holistic, energetic healing. Ancient systems of healing are much more knowledgeable of energetics and the pathways of expression. Because these systems are also immersed in ritual, spiritual belief and even psychospiritual issues, science has not yet found a way to apply itself to these mysteries and elusive systems.

As part of their philosophy, the Chinese educate themselves to understand nature in relation to themselves. The idea that the microcosm mirrors the macrocosm (and vice versa) allows the yin-yang fundamentals to be seen within the mind/body. For example, if the body is feeling symptoms of heat, excess yang has upset the balance, and a practitioner increases yin to cool the body back into balance. Such a simple dualistic system can also serve symptoms of the mind (i.e., excess yang causes symptoms such as restlessness, anxiety, etc.) or even explain environmental changes or social changes. In other words, this practical yin-yang philosophy is a multidimensional symbol that relates to all aspects of creation. The use of such a system can be easy to learn and can provide a good foundation for listening and understanding ourselves in relation to the world around us.

Using our senses with clarity and developing our ability to understand the energetic messages of mind/ body feedback loops gives us the opportunity to take action for corrective change. This is one function of communication: *to bring information to consciousness and thus giving us the freedom of choice.* Without communication, there can be no flow of energy and, hence, no evolutionary change.

An even more fundamental process of self-communication is our innate ability to just "know." We all use our intuitive perceptive abilities to create a sense of knowing. These abilities may have originally developed as a means of sensing danger, taking protective action, or preparing for environmental stress, such as drought, flood or disease. Intuition may be an inner voice or a subtle feeling. It can come in dreams or while we are awake—virtually at any time. It does not require intelligence, education or even physiological stability (though these may contribute to it); it can be some "opening of a window" to the nonlocal mind. The messages that our intuition gives to our conscious mind are a form of communication that permits us an opportunity of choice.

Usually there are two steps. The first is perceiving the extrasensory information, while the second is making the choice or decision. Sometimes these two steps seem combined into a state of being, where we just *know* what to do or we become conscious of just doing. This is a highly efficient function of consciousness that furthers evolution and personal and social growth.

Inner Dialogue

One of the ways we communicate with ourselves is through *inner dialogue*. We all talk to ourselves, whether it is to think through a problem, to find the appropriate words for a conversation, or to call attention to a particular experience or feeling.

Thought has various levels of manifestation, from the most subtle level to the spoken word. Most of us operate on the most superficial level, using language as our primary medium of communication. The words written on this page come from that surface level of thought. But what happens as we move our attention to deeper levels of thought? We notice a change in the format and quality of our thoughts. The format, or the "environmental setting" of the thought, moves from a linear, tightly-knit organization into a more expansive, less rational and more symbolic level. We see this difference when we compare waking state with the dream state. The deeper we go, the more dimensions of consciousness we traverse. The mind expands beyond our familiar three-dimensional reality.

Since thought and feeling are different vibrations of energy, the deeper we go, the more we "peel the onion" of emotion. We go to a more fundamental experience of feeling as we journey to the core of our life. To open to these subtle levels of self is to open communication to previously hidden aspects and to provide that information to consciousness in the present moment. The more we are aware, the easier it is to evaluate proper action. But this is not just a mental exercise; it also relates to the development of the intuition. That subtle feeling of the heart that just "knows" is one way that the Higher Self guides us. (This unfoldment of spiritual communication is discussed in Chapter 5.) Whenever we open the doors deep within, the experience will affect change. Our reality, which was previously based on the surface levels of life, now becomes more expanded and holistic. Since the microcosm mirrors the macrocosm, our inner reality shows us the outer reality, culminating in the experience of infinity. We may start in a state of constriction and shutdown, but through the process of communication, by expanding our consciousness and following our "knowing," we ultimately come full circle and are communing again with our source.

Witnessing

Intuition is primarily a right-brain function that speaks to us without the need to rationally think, evaluate, or make sense of the message. It can be as ordinary as choosing one color shirt over another on a given day. Much of our decision-making is spontaneous, without a lot of calculation. As we develop intuition, our inner dialogue brings more of this functioning to our consciousness. Instead of just doing, we begin to watch this refinement of activity unfold. This is called *witnessing*.

At first, we are just aware of the mind thinking thoughts; this leads to choices which, through an act of will, create a desired action. We watch the sequence of the phenomena unfold from desire to fulfillment, full of twists and turns, with abundant emotion, and sometimes surprise. The senses bring the story to us through the symbolic movie screen of our consciousness. Our witnessing consciousness watches, quietly, like a spectator in a theater. The spectator who witnesses *is consciousness*. It is that pure being which is beyond ego or personality-self, beyond that part of us that feels, chooses, or takes action. As the silent witness develops, more and more of life flows through our mind/body without obscuring or overshadowing the Self, which is synonymous with pure consciousness. When this witness is permanently experienced, we have self-realization, a state of cosmic consciousness.

In summary, the process of communication with ourselves is an evolving phenomenon. We start with listening to the body tell us what it is feeling and what it needs. By educating ourselves, we can expand our understanding of mind/body, diagnose a little more clearly and take effective action more efficiently.

One of the most important components in this process is the emotional body. Here we hold potent defense mechanisms that tend to push us toward control and shutdown. Our energetic memories of the past create and perpetuate layers of separation that block us from clear communication with ourselves and our environment. Our inner dialogue is the beginning of an evolutionary process of opening communication to deeper, more subtle levels of experience, ultimately bringing us into communion with the Infinite.

If we do have this silent witness within, this consciousness of Self, why does it seem so elusive, so intangible? Why is our experience of it so different than our everyday reality? Why isn't it like a normal object of perception? Why is it so difficult for the mind to understand? If it is nonlocal and universal, what blocks us from knowing it in daily life? And lastly, how can we hear its voice and communicate with it?

Dr. Larry Dossey in his book, *Recovering the Soul*, discusses these questions. As he puts it, "...our sense of our own universality is obscured by the physical constraints of the body."[1] The boundaries of the body, that is, its material form existing within time, are formidable restrictions to the perception of things that are intangible, unbounded, and beyond time. These characteristics of human life create a "wall" of separation from the spiritual realms. The senses connect us to what is happening outside of ourselves in the ever-changing world of phenomena. Manifest creation keeps the senses busy with plenty of stimuli. As long as there is activity, there will be constraints of time and matter.

The Memory of Suffering

There is another reason we are blocked from the soul. Having entered the game of life, we naturally hold onto form, repeatedly. The nature of karma *is* repetition. It requires the perpetuation of familiar forms, patterned responses, limited perspectives—in other words, *memory*. Memory can be held physically or energetically, deep within the subtle bodies of our personal field. Practically speaking, the difficulty of karmic memory is that it holds the emotional energy of the past and creates themes of repetitive expression. It starts with the initial imprint of our separation from God and snowballs into familiar feelings such as fear, anger, isolation, helplessness, and victimization. *Separation creates the suffering of life.*

The actual reason we don't commune with Spirit is because of the emotional memory of our past suffering and our unwillingness to open to it for fear of feeling the pain again. We have an ego that is required to keep those doors closed for protection, to insure and secure the present as it flows into the future. The future then becomes structured by the repressed memories of the past. This creates the illusion of fear and an expectation of continued suffering. We become attached to time. Our past is purposely forgotten, our future is controlled to the best of our ability, and our present loses its potential for free expression and continued expansion.

Our body holds the memory of karma and our attachment to it blocks us from knowing our Universal Self. By identifying with the body, our ego thinks we are the form and the feelings, so it insulates us in order to preserve our limited self-concept. On one level, it tries to protect us from suffering, if not from annihilation. On another level, its attachments keep us within boundaries, resisting the call for liberation. It fears unboundedness, which is equated with death, with nothingness. The ego is pledged to maintain self-identity, for this means continued existence. This vicious closed cycle is maintained by the fear of letting go of the past, thereby perpetuating form and time.

The emotional imprints of the past are powerful; they create form, and they create obstacles to our ability to listen clearly and know ourselves. Fortunately, *the releasing of past memory dissolves form.* As we heal and release the past, the boundaries loosen, the sense of self expands, the ego experiences greater freedom and we begin to realize the Universal Self. Lowering our "personal wall" opens up our feelings and allows for greater intimacy, which eventually leads us into communion. But first we must face the challenges of our past and communicate with the memories of our past choices in order to learn the lessons completely.

One of the most difficult yet most empowering lessons is about suffering. Suffering is caused by the separation from Universal Self. The greater the apparent gap, the more attachment our "ignore-ance" has in our emotional body. As consciousness opens, our memories of suffering come up and we are given the opportunity, once again, to deal with our hindrances and transform them into growth. Penetrating the walls to our inner communication can then be seen as the chance to experience new freedom.

The Body Speaks—A Session with Lia

Lia: *I seem to be very aware of my body. I feel my breathing settling down into a nice rhythm. I feel the body letting go of tension. I feel connected, at ease.*

Now I seem to be moving to the organs. I feel the lungs working, the heart beating, my stomach and intestines still processing. And I realize these organs are not separate and independent. They are part of my whole; they are me, yet not all of me. The air I breathe, the food I eat become part of me, part of my energy. The question comes: were these things part of me before? I see them become me now, but have the molecules been part of me before? The larger question seems to connect me to the big picture, the flow and cycles of energy....

My body says the intuition is accurate, the feeling validated.

Now, if the organs are part of me, then the tissues and cells are part of who I am. Each has its various functions, some quite different and unique, a collection of diverse forms and functions.

(Lia's body convulses in a series of muscular shivers running through her body for about two minutes.)

Oh, my God! My body is speaking to me, it's teaching me the physical relationships. It's as if the intelligence within my body is communicating with me.

If the body is the universe, the different levels of form and function are like the galaxies, solar systems, planets—you know, the subsets of the whole. The bone cell has its function and reality which is different than that of the nerve cell, though they are both cells, which is different than the liver organ, which is different than the respiratory system and so on.

This is incredible....

Yet they are all parts of me, of my wholeness. Each

performing their programmed function, yet they interrelate to the whole—like the brain being the boss that manages the factory. But there's an intelligence that's contained within and around the whole. Or we could say it's a spiritual consciousness that's omnipresent. It's not the brain or a function of the brain, but it exists there with the brain or the nerve cell or liver cell or any part. It's not physical, but on a spiritual dimension....

Now I see the tremendous variety of form and function. I see the old cells, the new cells, sick cells, dead cells, some cells that victimize others, some that mutate and change the rules of the program, some that are weak, and others seemingly invincible. But, as the whole, they are self-contained, and the body goes through its cycles and changes constantly, depending on the continual flux of activity governed by the overseeing intelligence. It's clear that the spiritual intelligence doesn't change; it's just there, just witnessing all the activity. I see that sometimes the activity gets chaotic and overshadows the awareness of the intelligence, and at other times, the activity gets into a state of clarity and an orderliness of function. Then the intelligence is perfectly seen and felt.

This intelligence is natural law. It seems to hold it all together and makes life work.

But what of the role of the emotions? The body tells me that this is another aspect of my wholeness. It's not like cells and organs, but the cells correspond to experiences, memories, even genetic instincts which create feelings. The feelings create systems of response—I'd guess you call it behavior. Behaviors become habituated systems that define aspects of our personality and our sense of ego, our likes and dislikes, our state of reality. Mind and programmed thought are connected here too. This is so amazing. I've never had this perspective before; it's such a flow of information, a communication to who I am and what I'm made of. Yet it is also a communication to that omnipresent of intelligence, Spirit, whatever you want to call it....

Yet my ego says I am an entity that is different than another person, different than a tree, a cloud, a star. What the ego says is true: a liver cell is different than a nerve cell, yet they are all me. My life force enlivens them as God enlivens this form and function. I am part of God until I realize I am God, just as the liver cell becomes self-conscious that it is one with the whole.

As the ego expands its knowing, it realizes on one dimension it is different and simultaneously it knows it is part of a larger organism, a larger consciousness. Spiritually, we become aware that this organism requires different forms and functions to work together in harmony. Harmonizing differences is the job of intelligence.

Facilitator: How can you use this information in your personal life?

Lia: *Immediately I see that it helps me clear judgment and the illusion of separation....*

Before I was stuck in the concept of separation, a feeling that we should believe the same things, adopt similar behaviors—that being different was somehow wrong. That feeling of difference made it easy to judge right and wrong based on my programming of what morality should be. Growing up as a kid, the social pressure to conform was powerful; it molds you into a nice, agreeable little robot with conditioned responses. Any idiosyncrasy is dangerous within judgmental groups. I was a victim to that pervasive separation energy.

My body is teaching me by analogy.

Facilitator: What are the messages of this analogy?

Lia: *Well, I see that being different is important in the sense that everything has its form and function. I don't have to judge difference or judge different roles other than mine. All are equally important. For example, to shun the liver, we die. To shun the lungs, we die. To cut off or reject a part of ourselves is to weaken, limit, and kill the sum of the parts.*

I see that the micro mirrors the macro. My body is an analogy for the planet. Being an individual, I have felt like a unique entity among the masses, different and separate. This is the norm, the effect of the theme of separation. But now I see we are just part of a larger entity. The cosmic body is made up of different types of individual parts with different forms and functions. If we could really cognize this, we would treat others differently and the environment differently. We are not separate; we are one big organism. It's so clear to me now.

This cosmic organism has a multiplicity of characteristics. It has yin and yang, young and old, some healthy, some dying, some strong, some weak—everything is included in the whole. Even within the diversity are the differing roles. Some parts victimize other parts, some stay the same, others are constantly changing. But most do what they are programmed to do, while others stimulate new programming for change and evolution. There are a myriad of checks and balances as we see within the body. So it's true on the macro scale also. For example, when the body is sick and exhibits a fever, what happens? The fever is in its yang phase: a hot, high temperature, a holding of energy resulting from inflammation and stuckness, a high pressure within the system, a dryness within the symptoms, pain, anxiety, delirious consciousness, cellular death, chaos overriding. Then the balancing mechanism is triggered: yin. The fever "breaks," the water arrives as sweat to cool down the heat. The energy starts flowing, the body detoxes, releasing its impurities and chaos. The opening and clearing allow the system to come into a restful, more grounded state of activity.

These are all the qualities of yin balancing the excess of yang. Of course, there is time required after the crisis to bring optimum balance back to the system and to strengthen it. It's a time of rebuilding as the balance point swings to the center. But by going through the stress of the crisis, the body adapts to the "purpose" of the fever, and antibodies are created so the body is well prepared to handle any invasion in the future. So we have evolved to a more powerful condition. (Did you get all that?)

Facilitator: Absolutely! How is this an analogy for the planet?

Lia: *Well, of course! This is what our planet is going through. The yang sickness, which I've just described, and the need of the yin to bring it into balance. The feminine (yin) initiates the healing process in order to evolve the system into greater yang potential. Or we could say the Mother is teaching us how to find our balance and come out of illusion and back to the integration of unity consciousness. It's a great analogy. So we don't have to sit in judgment; instead we just need to get more conscious.*
     (End of session)

3

Healing Communication Behavior

The present condition of human communication is primitive. We may think that because of the development of high-tech machinery, fiber-optic communication networks, and the ability to see and hear into the far reaches of space that we must be quite advanced in the field of communication; after all AT&T guarantees that we can talk to natives in New Guinea. But all this is just technology that broadens our boundaries of the universe; it has little effect on our ability to listen with our heart to another being or, for that matter, to God/dess. Being able to clearly hear a voice overseas does not mean we are really listening to that soul. Hearing only means that the ear is perceiving sound. Real listening is conscious.

We are poor listeners most of the time. Even if we are listening, communication requires a medium of connection and the ability to make sense of the information that is being relayed. The language of the information must be processed (translated) into understanding. Language must be learned; if it is not, the result is thought to be a serious block to human development.

Since interpersonal communication is the flow and exchange of energy between people, it is not only a daily part of life but a necessity of life. We don't live on a deserted island. We need to communicate every day and, for most of us, it is the activity we engage in more than any other. Whenever we are with others, we are drawn into relationship and communication connects us to that relationship.

The dynamics of communication can be simplified. At any given moment, communication includes the one who is giving energy and the one who is receiving that energy. In his book *Between People*, Dr. John A. Sanford uses the analogy of playing catch. One person holds the ball and announces his intention to throw the ball to another. He goes through the motions and propels the ball into the waiting hands of the other. For the game to succeed, there must be some rules by which to play i.e.; 1) don't throw the ball until I'm ready to catch it; 2) don't throw it over my head; and 3) don't throw it too hard. In other words, in this game, let me treat you as I would like you to treat me. The game may last as long or as short a time as we both agree. If we can't agree, one or both of us may feel hurt. Then our emotional bodies get involved and add more difficulty to the process.

The object of the "communication" game is not to be competitive. It is not like tennis, in which we are trying to hit the ball so it can not be returned to us, or like football, where we must stop the person with the ball from reaching the goal. The purpose of communication is for *both* people to benefit: the one who gives feels fulfilled in the giving, and the one who receives feels fulfilled in receiving. When both people can give and receive, the process works perfectly. Likewise, in our spiritual life we have to be open to the flow of energy in both directions. We don't just demand of God/dess; we communicate so that we can both give and receive. We experience both sides of the coin in balance, and each side is full.

More practically, if someone is talking to us, we must not just hear them; we must be ready to listen and respond. This is a skill we learn. It requires the ability to be in the present moment and to be open to what the other wants to share with us. This is not always easy; many issues can block what seems to be a simple process. Do I even want to listen? Am I prepared to listen? Many times we assume the other is available, willing, and interested. Such assumptions may be based on false beliefs or empty wishes. Also, am I physiologically able to listen—am I fatigued or clearly attentive? For example, how many school children are really able to listen to their teacher on a hot, muggy day after a heavy lunch? Sometimes we ignore such simple causes for communication failure.

When someone lectures to us with no intention of listening to our response, after awhile we start shutting down because the energy is not completing its cycle. Such lecturing may be based in another person's agenda without agreement from the receiver, as in compulsory education. Lecturing that occurs in interpersonal relationships can often be an avoidance mechanism that blocks intimate connections, or it can be a defense mechanism to hide our fears.

Similarly, a person may make an announcement or declaration that requires no response: "I'm going home!" or "I have nothing else to say on that matter, case closed." We can feel cut off and disappointed with this type of communication. We may want to relate, but the other has unilaterally decided to shut down the communication process.

Because human beings are generally poor communicators, we have developed behaviors to compensate and protect ourselves from painful communication. How many times do we try to get our message across before we finally give up? It is common to see communication fail. It happens every day; it becomes habitual. The result is that we stop listening or we shut down emotionally. When we stop listening, we disconnect ourselves and withdraw from relationship or find something else to occupy our attention. It requires a certain degree of courage to open ourselves to communication because when we connect with another person it is not always pleasant. If we have been hurt often, communication becomes conditional and guarded, as if we were saying, "I will only listen to you if you promise not to say anything that will hurt me." Of course, this doesn't work because our initial fear about "what might happen" has already biased our ability to be open and receptive.

Sometimes a person approaches us as if they were wearing a baseball catcher's protective equipment—chest pad, face mask, shin guards, etc. They are so defensive that we can't quite find the real person underneath it all to whom we can relate. If the person is shut down or "absent," how do we connect with them? How do we connect with someone who is not available, whose behavior says, "I'm uninterested," "I'm afraid," or "Leave me alone?"

These few examples of difficult communication behavior demonstrate the complexity and broad spectrum of human communication. How do we learn to be successful in our communication when blockage and failure are the rule?

We must choose to be conscious and take the risk, even though we will be hurt from time to time. Our expectations may be shattered and it won't always be fun. The human heart breaks but the irony is that the heart is resilient and learns and grows stronger. The heart evolves through experience. We find that we do survive, that we can handle it, and that from our expanded spiritual viewpoint, it's all okay. Once we take this step and choose to be open, to be conscious, our intention and attitude can be adapted to help our situation.

Our intention plays an important role. Ideally, we make a conscious choice, with clear responsibility, to pursue relationship without conditions. When we set our intention to be present and available to someone, we fulfill our role as the listener, being openly attentive and receptive. Then we have accomplished our part of the partnership. Spiritually, we remain clear and unattached to the outcome.

The Dalai Lama once told me, "With pure intention, with a pure heart, go forward in action with no regret." If our intention is clearly to be there for someone, to be in relationship with an open heart, then anything can happen, and we can be free of regret. Karma will play out as it needs to. We don't need to be attached to the outcome. The process of communication allows the energy to flow for the purpose of playing itself out, and we face it openly and consciously. By our example, we demonstrate openness. Instead of shutdown, openness can become the norm. Instead of communication being conditional, it can be about honesty and trust. We can communicate our intention to be present, regardless of the response or action, because we *can* handle it. We don't want to be codependant— we don't need to promise or agree to take responsibility for the other person's behavior; but we can be available and we can be responsible for our *own* responses and feelings in this interaction.

Finding Our Voice

In order to speak, we must use the physical organs that give our thoughts the ability to make sounds and, thereby, project over distance. Our voice becomes the mechanism that allows our sound energy to reach out to the world. Because our voice uses vibrational energy as its vehicle, it carries many subtle levels of information and feeling into relationship.

Esoterically, our voice holds within it the seeds of our karmic history. Imprints of memory from the past are constantly conveyed by our speech. A simple example is language. Language is a behavior. We practice it and use it repeatedly. Voice is one way we express the behavior of language, but on a deeper emotional level, the behavioral aspect of language holds imprints, associations, and other memories of how we reacted to our interpersonal relationships of the past.

One male client discovered that growing up with a loud, angry, and demonstrative father affected his voice and communication behavior. He reacted to this negative yang behavior by withdrawing and becoming silent and mute. After an incident with any loud, angry person, he noticed that his voice would crack and he could only talk in a high-pitched falsetto until the emotional reaction subsided.

If reincarnation is valid, then we've probably spoken many languages and lived through every type of lifetime as members of every race. Voice holds a multidimensional quality—it forms a characteristic of the persona and to some extent, we identify with it as we have in other lives, carrying that quality of our identity forward. Within that very same voice, we also hold our *true* voice, the voice of our spirit. This voice is neither male nor female but is the voice of God/dess, the sound of Creation mixed with the silence of the emptiness. Since our voice is an outer expression of our inner reality, it becomes another window into our emotional body programming. Because it is hard to hear ourselves with any degree of sensitivity, many of our karmic patterns remain unconscious. Or they may be so familiar that we take them for granted.

Our accent, style of speech, word choice, tonal quality, and range of voice all come from our previous models of relationship. Imitating others' vocal behavior acts as the catalyst for developing our own speech patterns. Yet not only do we mimic the superficial aspects of speech, we also copy and absorb much of the subtler levels of communication from our relationships—usually from family members. For example, how did Father express affection? How did he voice his frustration, irritation or disagreement? How did Mother voice her disappointments or dreams? How did she express humor?

Being the children of our parents as well as being influenced by other role models, we have acquired our voices and behaviors from a willingness to imitate others. On the other hand, our voices may reflect the development of a behavior that expresses the polar-opposite energy of our parents. We tend to internalize those behaviors that will elicit the responses of the past. Our voice will always be an expression of our past imprints until we have cleared the energetic attachments of our emotional imprinting. Then, and only then, will we find our Universal Self and our true voice of self-expression.

As I work with clients at the Deva Foundation, I often notice changes in their voices. Not long ago, a woman called home to talk to her husband. After a week of sessions, she said it was so strange because it took him a minute or so before he recognized who he was talking to. She had opened her true voice, which now had a new range and tonal characteristics that had been previously blocked.

Self-Image, the Changing World of the Persona

One aspect of voice is the persona it expresses. To a certain extent, we will try to create a voice that is a reflection of who we want to be. I've noticed that certain people will exaggerate an accent or use different words as the topic of discussion changes. One member of my family, when talking about our family heritage, would shift from clear, unaccented English into an aristocratic East-Coast accent with a touch of snobbishness. This would quickly shift into a Texas twang when some "good ol' boys" walked into the room.

This may be seen often in adolescents who are maturing into young men and women and searching for a concept of self. I remember one of my high school friends, who, being very insecure and always seeking acceptance and approval, would change his accent dramatically every month to adapt to a new group of peers. The formulation of our persona can be watched through the changes in voice and the type of language we adopt. To be a legitimate member of a street gang may require the construction of a unique dialect or slang. It gives the person a sense of connection but, at the same time, can separate them from others, which also may be part of the desired scenario.

As we grow up, there may come a time when we judge our past vocal behavior because it doesn't fit with who we want to be in the present—a Pygmalion syndrome. After a behavior is locked in, it can be hard to change. This is certainly true for the persona. Only our spirit can release us from the illusion of our persona—who we think we are then transforms into who we *really* are. Unfortunately, we move through stages of programming from our parents and society that pressure us into what they think we should be, including how to speak properly. Then years later, ironically we go into therapy to unlearn all these behaviors in order to reveal our natural being and how to express it authentically.

Stress and Busyness

Living a rushed life-style makes communication even more difficult, because we fail to listen. This failure to communicate is not only damaging to relationships, but it also carries a cloud of inefficiency and failure into the activities of life. Unfortunately, the following story is a familiar one:

"Joe, hurry up! You're going to be late for work, again," Jill, his wife, screams from the kitchen. She's a little perturbed with Joe's habit of sleeping late so that he's always in a rush in the morning.

Meanwhile, as he gets dressed for work, Joe is still feeling the effects of a restless night and the cloud of grogginess in his head. He feels a lack of energy and is upset by his wife's nagging as he gets dressed for work. "Why does she always get upset with me in the morning?" He wonders. "I usually get to work on time."

At this point, Joe's five-year-old daughter walks into the bedroom carrying her new tennis shoes.

"Daddy, can you help me tie my shoelaces? I can't remember how to do this."

"Honey, ask your mother to help you; I'm late for work," Joe says as he rushes past her with a quick pat on the head. Jill scowls, her hands on her hips, and Joe knows what's coming before she says a word.

"You drive me crazy every morning with this last-minute rush. I fixed you breakfast and now you're going to tell me you're sorry but that you've got to get to work. Why do you do this to us?"

"I just didn't sleep well last night; it will be different from now on, I promise," Joe pleads.

"But you always say that," she says with frustration. "And by the way, on your way home can you pick up the dry cleaning and next door to the cleaners is that new pasta store; I want you to pick up the cheese ravioli I ordered for dinner tonight with your boss. Make sure you pick it up by six o'clock, because that's when they close and I don't have anything else to cook, and..."

As Jill goes on, Joe is feeling the stress of the morning and he can't remember where he put his car keys. "I thought I put them in my briefcase," but he can't find them. While she's talking about the cleaners, he's trying to remember if he wore his overcoat yesterday. "Maybe I left the keys in the pocket." And, "Which cleaners does she use? Didn't we switch cleaners after they lost my new suit?"

"Ah, here are my keys in my overcoat! I've got to run, love, I'll pick up the cleaning—see you later." He rushes out the door while Jill is still talking.

"Joe, dinner is at 7:30, so come home on time and pick up

a bottle of good red wine. You know how your boss loves good wine," she shouts as Joe slams the car door.

Frustrated, Jill exclaims to herself, "What kind of relationship is this? I can't remember the last time we could just sit down and have a nice romantic dinner." She slumps into the sofa and tears run down her face as she realizes that once again, Joe hasn't heard a word she's said all morning.

Jill's right. Joe arrives at seven o'clock with the cleaning in his hand but no pasta and no wine. When she calmly explains what her instructions were that morning, all Joe can say is, "You didn't say a word about picking up pasta or wine!" He is angry and yet deep inside he knows it's true. And it isn't the first time this has happened.

This is a common story. The details may differ from couple to couple, but the dynamics are universal. There are many themes at work in this vignette. The first, which sets the stage for disaster, is the habitual stress of busyness, which we can call "the rushing." Part of Joe's addiction to rushing to work is his accumulated stress and his inability to rest adequately to alleviate his fatigue. The rushing is a desperate attempt to override his predicament but, of course, it will always fail. Denial and control are only temporary measures to ward off the inevitable closing down of consciousness. Their secondary effect will be to make relationship virtually impossible. Joe's mental cloudiness causes him to be unavailable and self-absorbed, and it creates more stress in the process.

Another major theme due to his clouded and agitated awareness is Joe's inability to be in tune with what's really important in his life—namely his family relationships. From a spiritual point of view, the karma of a relationship is almost always the highest priority, family being at the top of the list. Joe is caught in the busyness of the world, and it not only blocks him from meaningful and intimate communication with his loved ones but it also closes the door to the fullness of the present moment. Only in the present moment can we truly know our Self.

Joe is working on a vital lesson of life and his approach is not uncommon: *take the lesson to the extreme and learn it harshly*. We could predict that if Joe doesn't realize what's happening and break the pattern, the pattern will break him through the disintegration of his family, work, and, eventually, the collapse of his health. When Joe hits rock bottom, then maybe he can build a new life, but it will be hard, given the tragedy and loss he will have experienced by then. Wouldn't it be easier to learn the lesson a bit earlier and save all the suffering?

Reactivity of the Emotional Body: The Challenge of Communicating

The main purpose of communication is to bring us into relationship. Usually, how we initiate our connection with another will determine how the process will unfold. If our intention is to be open and available, then we can prepare ourself to be attentive to the other, hopefully without judgment. If we carry through with this beginning, the other person will not be triggered defensively and will respond in a like manner. If the other perceives that we are listening and that he or she is being heard, then that person can open up to listening to us.

As we know, this process can quickly disintegrate. One of the most difficult situations to handle is when another person throws us the energy of a potent emotion within their words. Anger, rage, or any of the other "negative yang" feelings are so powerful that we usually react quickly by withdrawing or defending ourselves, or by responding with a similar attack.

Projected anger has a tendency to elicit anger in ourselves, quickly inhibiting our ability to communicate. But if we can be conscious and recognize what is happening, we may be able to bypass our old patterns of reactivity. In Buddhist mindfulness training, the instruction would be to return to the breath. This works because, energetically, an attack has the effect of paralyzing our energy, causing our breath to stop or become uneven and short. Focusing on the breath stabilizes the flow of energy and diverts the tendency to react. It focuses our energy on the need to return to Self, which will balance and expand our consciousness. Focusing on our breath immediately prepares us to respond positively.

We must respond to and communicate with the angry person. It may not be desirable to withdraw; this is symbolic of shutdown or running away from unpleasantness. Admittedly, sometimes this may be our only option if our attempt to communicate hits a brick wall of judgment or violence. Then all we can do is let it go and honor the other's choice of anger and our choice not to engage them.

We can acknowledge the other person's emotions: "I know you are angry"; or "Tell me why you are angry"; or "Help me understand your anger." These words sometimes help to break through a difficult moment. Acknowledging the other's feelings and encouraging the release of negative energy may clear the air enough to reestablish the possibility of a continued discussion. Of course, our habits of communication may not permit us such an "enlightened" response, yet we always have the ability to change, to find a more successful way of relating. At first, consciousness is required, along with an intention of "nonviolence" and the courage to transcend the other's judgment, fear, and pain. This is an opportunity to meet anger with the open heart of compassion. If we can demonstrate this new behavior, it will not only strengthen our new found ability, but we will also model it for the other person. The more of us who exemplify new behavior, the greater effect we will have on world consciousness. That's how life evolves.

A more difficult situation is when we are triggered subtly through a disguised or oblique suggestion that carries with it a passive-aggressive energy. The innuendo seems to hit us squarely in the solar plexus, yet we never saw it coming—we have no chance to defend ourselves. Most of the time we just react—maybe not in anger but in defensiveness, withdrawal, sadness, or guilt. The other person has successfully triggered us and their subtle "victimizer" role is fulfilled. It may have started with a look or with the judgmental energy behind a meaningless or neutral word, but the intention soon becomes obvious.

Sometimes we use passive/aggressive behavior to hurt, insult, or project our own judgment and pain onto another. We may not permit ourselves overt aggression, so we play it out subtly, yet the effect is the same. The consequences are just as harsh, if not worse. It's also a great way to avoid taking responsibility for our actions because it is easy to deny that we are being the victimizer. Manipulation of this sort is quite common. If we are often the victim of it, we become conditioned to distrust communication of any sort; we feel vulnerable all the time and retreat into shutdown.

As we can see, when the emotional body gets triggered and emotions get tangled up in the communication process, things get complicated. Many people are uncomfortable with feelings and may react in ways that attempt to either "get control" or bypass the emotions at hand. One common tendency is to use argument as a way of getting out of the emotions and into the mind, where we may think, "I should be logical and rational in order to resolve this predicament."

"You shouldn't feel that way!" is a great way to dismiss communication by invalidating the emotions at hand. Emotion is usually part of communication because it is part of the energy we are conveying to the other. True communication reveals to the other who we are at this moment. It is honest, having no need to hide feelings but trusting enough to put ourself "out there," emotions and all. When we open our communication to include emotion, we are truly expressing ourselves. That honest expression benefits our situation and provides a supportive environment in which to evolve.

Looking Deeper: The Case of Alex

Judgment denies the existence of God/dess. If I judge myself, I negate the God/dess within me. If I judge another, I deny that person's divinity. Because judgment denies the godliness within all things, it creates a wall of separation. This energy of divisiveness is inherently destructive and will eventually harm any personal or social relationship. Since the theme of separation is the basis of all karmic expression, pain and suffering arise from the loss of one's unity with the God-source. The following session illustrates not only the effects of separation/judgment in relationship, but takes it to its karmic source in a past life (or symbolic story).

Alex wanted to work on his dysfunctional relationship with women, especially his feeling of being victimized by his wife and through his mother's alcoholism. Alex, a devout Catholic, also felt a deep sense of nonspecific guilt which he associated with his religion.

Alex: *I feel so much negativity toward my wife. It's a combination of anger, anxiety, and profound disappointment— you could say a lot of judgment. So I can't talk to her, and even if I could, she never listens to me.*

Facilitator: How do you see her now? Bring her into focus.

Alex: *She's a witch with an aura of fire. You can't get close to her or you'll get burned with her cruelty. It reminds me of times when my mother would be drunk. Even her words are like a stream of fire; they pierce me like swords. I feel so much pain in our interactions; there's no communication. Even when we try to start to talk, we get off on the wrong foot. I pull away or she subtly criticizes me, and then we can't recapture our intention to try to work things out.*

Maybe our intention isn't clear either...(Tears).... She doesn't know how to say something without triggering me. I have trouble with her "shoulds" and I just back off, shut down. Then if I do try to respond, she interrupts me. Do you know how irritating that is? I can never finish my thought before she jumps in there with her self-righteous viewpoint, or she changes the subject or confuses me with some intellectual bullshit that makes no sense whatsoever.... She has no patience with me. Before long she has lost her temper, then I react by losing mine, and we literally become possessed—both screaming at each other....(Rapid breathing, tension throughout the body)....

Facilitator: Feel the energy in the body. Go into it.

Alex: *I just see the same pattern—just like I described—we really do the same thing over and over.*

You know, I don't think we ever really get to the issue. It's as if we are just caught in the smoke of it and our emotional game-playing is a way to deny or maybe avoid the real issue.

Facilitator: Ask your Higher Self to take you to the source of the smoke, to the deeper issue within you.

Alex: *The word that keeps coming is "respect." I don't think she respects me—all I feel is her judgment....*

I see some imagery, maybe like a past life. I see a church, like in France—very ornate, tall steeples, a bell ringing. I see a priest dressed in white robes walking next to a novice—he must be sixteen or seventeen years old. He's an attractive young man—clear eyes, a look of innocence, yet angry somehow; and I'm the older priest, maybe 40. It looks like we've just finished a wedding. The young bride is crying. She's one of the devout parishioners; she's here almost every day. She does a lot of volunteer work for the church. I can't tell if she's crying out of happiness or if she's sad. As she walks out, I feel a constriction in my stomach. There's some past connection here; it doesn't feel good....

Facilitator: Move into that feeling, see what the connection is.

Alex: *I don't see anything... I just feel afraid.*

Facilitator: Feel it. What are you afraid of?

Alex: *I'm afraid to look at her... I know I'm blocking it, but I feel that I was in love with her... I see us having sex. After sex I felt so guilty—that I had created the worst sin imaginable. How could I do that? I was like her father. She was just eighteen or nineteen. My stomach is cramping....*

Facilitator: Take it forward. What happened?

Alex: *She felt guilty, too, and I made it worse because I told her it was a sin and that God would punish the sinful. God, I made it sound like it was her fault!*

I avoided her. I wouldn't talk to her. Every time she would come into the church I'd go in the back room and lock the door. And she'd cry. This went on for weeks. Then I didn't see her for a month or so, until she showed up one morning, very early. I was teaching some class with the three young novices and she interrupted us and demanded to see me, so I couldn't avoid her. She said that she was pregnant. She said that the local midwife knew, too. I was shocked. I started screaming at her. I told her she was being punished and to leave the church. I was scared to death, but all I could do was be angry at her; it was her fault....

Ah, now I see. The young novice heard what happened. He must have been listening through the door. He knew what I had done. Now I had destroyed two people that I had loved, the girl and now the novice.

I told her she must never tell and that she must marry if she was to avoid scandal. And she did three weeks later. She married some simpleminded kid who didn't know anything about sex or pregnancy. She had the baby and everyone thought it was his. Except for the novice who knew and hated me for it. I had betrayed his trust and respect. He never forgave me. He left the church soon after the baby was born. He rejected the church and me, and it was all my fault. Both souls were lost to the church—damned, but not like me. God would punish me with greater harshness, because I deserved it...(Coughing)... *I died only a few years later.*

Facilitator: How did you die?

Alex: *I choked on some meat or a bone, something caught in my throat.*

Facilitator: Ask if there's anything else you need to see?

Alex: *Well, I've known all along that the novice is my wife and* *the young girl I impregnated is my mother. The girl could not handle the overshadowing guilt and she became an alcoholic. She tried to shutdown the pain, but her child and husband suffered terribly.*

Facilitator: Anything else?

Alex: *My Higher Self says that because of my self-judgment I have been afraid to be honest with my feelings because I've felt my wife really hates me, that I wasn't honest with my love in that life and I'm not honest now—yet I'm afraid to lose her again.... But Higher Self says both women really do love me. Underneath all the shit, all they want is to be loved—honestly....*
(End of session)

This session is a good example of the psychodynamics of separation/judgment and its effect on the emotional body and communication. The emotional body was not able to break the age-old patterning of its karmic attachments, and any attempt to communicate met with the same energies being expressed. Alex realized that he was back in the old familiar pattern, but he needed to repeat it one more time before it was obvious. When we're caught in the middle of it, there is no way to stop it. Most of the time, it will run its course. But there will be a time when we can step out of the self-absorption and into consciousness; then we can transform the situation and clear the energy. Alex proceeds to do that by going into the symbolism of a past lifetime.

Alex's experience is one of judgment, both internal and external. As a priest, he commits the "sin" of sexual intercourse out of wedlock which is also a violation of his vow of celibacy. Then he projects his guilt toward the very one he has fallen in love with. Out of his pain, he hurts the two people closest to him. He cannot handle the emotional pressure, so he internalizes it, withdraws, and avoids any reminder of what he's done by shutting down communication. He seals his fate and quickly dies via the shutdown of the throat chakra. His judgment kills him.

In this lifetime, Alex chose the soul he had loved, yet blamed, as his mother. She was still a woman but in a new role, in which he feels the anger of the past expressed toward him in a love/hate relationship. He feels that much of his difficulty with his mother in this lifetime stems from the issues of that past life—namely, judgment, control, nonspecific anger (especially when she was intoxicated and out of her mother role), and yet a profound sense of neediness arising out of the loneliness.

The issues with lover/mother were then projected upon his lover/wife in this lifetime, and she reacts by rejecting it. She didn't want to be a mirror for his unresolved mother issues, but because of her judgment, she was part of the communication problem. When I asked Alex if the feeling of not being respected was ever discussed with his wife, he said no. He had assumed that his wife didn't respect him and this issue was seen proven in the symbolism of the past life. I then helped him to see that even in his past life, it was assumed and not actually discussed, and that this theme of assuming (rather than communicating) was also being repeated today.

The emotional body creates its own reality and can use assumptions and biased perceptions to fuel its attachment to that reality. Because of Alex's self-judgment—he saw himself as a sinner who was being punished—he didn't respect himself. But that may not be the reality for others in his life. Perhaps they feel anger, disappointment, or profound sadness. They may even see him with compassion. Assumptions rarely have anything to do with reality. Alex, because of his fear and shutdown, was not able to find the truth of his situation until now. By energetically releasing his attachment to these symbolic themes, he was able to approach his wife and mother with greater openness and clarity. They responded differently, and now communication is possible. As a result, they are clearing the emotional barriers between them. Alex is happier and his relationship with his wife is growing stronger.

4

Sexual Communication: Union with Another

Communication creates relationship. At the core of interpersonal relationships is the instinctual genetic demand for survival through procreation. In order for the species to survive, there must be sexual union giving rise to new life. Yet the human species and several other animals (such as dolphins) have transcended the survival-only need for sex. Instead of sex being only for procreation, humans have allowed it to become an experience of enjoyment and intimate connection.

Communication, essentially, is both a flow of energy that connects us to others and a multidimensional interaction that opens us to infinite possibilities. Therefore, human communication is active and requires consciousness to complete its purpose. Without the process of communication, relationship would not be viable because the connection could not be made. The flow of energy between two people opens up all possibilities for the sharing of information and intelligence, and therefore is essential to life even on the most fundamental level. In order for the atoms of hydrogen (H_2) and oxygen (O_2) to combine to create the water molecule (H_2O), there must be an interaction. We could say the hydrogen and oxygen communicate, which allows their energy to be shared and a change of state results. The same thing happens when the egg and the sperm connect; change results and evolution takes another step forward. Without that flow of energy and the dynamics of interaction, life would cease to exist; the cosmic dance of energy and intelligence would dissolve into non-activity.

Sexual energy is one of the most powerful energies within us, yet socially it is enshrouded in judgment, dysfunction, and misunderstanding. Because of its power, religions and oftentimes our parents have tried to regulate it through moral laws; governments have followed suit; and educational institutions have failed to teach young people how to handle this energy and use it successfully.

Issues within society have their basis within the issues of the individual. Our personal sexual issues are deeply imprinted from lifetimes of sexual misuse and abuse. As we become more conscious of the multidimensional power and use of sexual energy and heal our personal history of sexual experience, we can then expand and refine this important part of being human.

For sexual energy to reach its highest expression, we must take our communication with our partner to its ultimate—*the merging into communion.* This sacred act of nature that conceives new life from the joining of yin and yang contains the power of creation, which manifests progressive forms, ideas, and new life. God/dess is manifested again and again, bringing the divine into form. The sexual act can produce the ecstasy of that communion.

Pathways of Sexual Energy

Esoterically, at the moment of creation, yin and yang, the fundamental polarities of life, arise from the unboundedness of the Absolute and communicate to create "the ten thousand things" as discussed in Chinese philosophy. There is nothing in creation that is only yin or only yang, but each embraces the other. In the deepest darkness of yin lies the spark of light of yang. In the driest desert of yang there is a molecule of moisture of yin. Yin and yang are destined to mix, interact, and manifest all levels of creation. Wherever there is manifestation, there is the dance of yin and yang. To recognize this is to see our part in the dance. The purpose of the dance is to move in such harmony and with such perfect timing that the two dancers are seen as one, perfectly synchronized, until the two merge into transcendental unity, into communion. This is both the ultimate purpose and the path of life—communication into communion.

In Chinese medical philosophy, the kidney energy rules the sexual energy. The kidney meridian originates at the bottom of the little toe, running under the foot to the medial side, through the heel, and ascending the medial side of the leg and thigh, through the groin to the tailbone, and internally entering the kidney organ. One internal branch continues upward until it reaches the root of the tongue. Another internal branch communicates with the bladder and reemerges as the surface meridian, running upward past the navel just lateral to the midline, through the breast, and ending below the clavicle. Another internal branch moves from the lungs, joins the heart, and flows into the breast to connect with the pericardium meridian. *(See diagram next page).*

The reason this description is important is to show, both physically and energetically, the pathways of the kidney energy and therefore the sexual energy. The sexual energy not only impacts the sexual organs but energetically connects at the base of the spine (the source of kundalini), influencing the lumbar area, the bladder and sexual organs, the liver, the diaphragm, the lungs, the pericardium, and the heart.

All of these acupuncture meridian systems have energetically important functions—for example, the lungs are the master controller of all the energy in the body. Therefore, the sexual act stimulates and moves energy powerfully throughout the body as a whole, opening the energy for

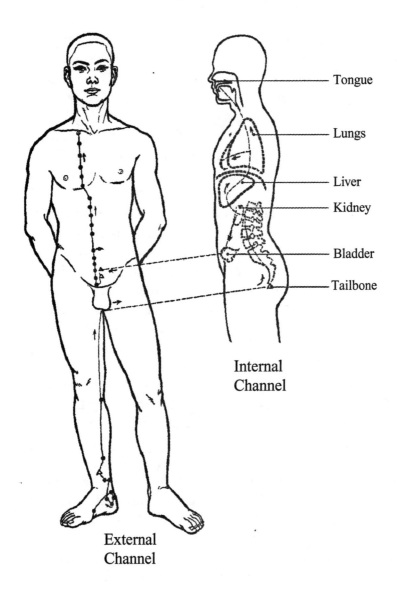

Tongue

Lungs

Liver

Kidney

Bladder

Tailbone

Internal
Channel

External
Channel

The Kidney Meridian

From: *An Outline of Chinese Acupuncture*, pg. 48, Foreign Language
Press, Peking, 1915

"conception." This is true whether the man liberates his yang (sperm), whether the woman opens her yin to receive the yang (the egg receiving the sperm), or whether the man and woman are both giving and receiving energy, emotion, and creativity in order to merge and become one.

Chinese medicine includes the concept of six different levels or dimensions of energy within the mind/body. From the superficial to the subtle, the kidney energy shares in the deepest level with the heart energy. Being the deepest and most subtle, we are describing the kidney and heart as energetically the most yin of the body. Obviously, the relationship between the kidney and heart is most intimate; one directly affects the other. The kidney energy must touch the heart energy, and vice versa. Emotionally, the kidneys have a tendency to hold the karma of fear, which partially explains why we may constrict the heart for fear of being hurt. But, more profound than that is the fear of true intimacy which requires the letting go of our ego-constraints resulting in the transcendence of the boundaries of self. This is the difficult challenge of energetic communion. Yet, as we overcome this resistance, the fulfillment is unbounded.

To ease the emotional body's resistance, the kidney energy must nourish the heart. One way this is done is through the sexual energy. But again, fear holds the sexual energy at bay; the heart defends against losing itself or being overwhelmed by emotion. As a result, the ego maintains its theme of separation. When the heart doesn't open, the energy doesn't flow. Full expression of sexual union can occur only with a combination of both the love of the heart and the sexual energy of the kidney. If the heart is not open and its energy does not flow upward to clear the separation/judgment of the throat chakra, we maintain these themes and their limiting effects.

When we surrender to the sacred sexual act, we truly experience the wonder of a multidimensional experience. The sexual energy awakens and reaches out to draw the lover close. The energy moves and builds, and the "dance" of communication expands consciousness. We tune into the other as we tune into ourselves. The kidney energy enlivens the kundalini; we feel the base of the spine begin to energize, and that energy starts to flow up the spine. On a physical level, this energy activates the nervous system, and messages are sent for arousal. We could call this the "quickening." The liver and kidney meridians send their energy to the sexual organs. As the energy moves up through the system, the lungs empower the rest of the body (the breathing rate increases), and the heart reaches out to connect with our partner. The heart and kidneys have prepared the way for communication.

Awareness is thrilled in the relationship of love, affection, and the intermingling of so many energies. If our karma is relatively clear and we are emotionally open, all of our fear is gone and our energy flows uninhibitedly. The heart expands; its joy and love circulate throughout the body. The heart chakra allows the flow of spirit to move up to the throat chakra. At this point, communication progresses into merging. The flow of energy clears the separation/judgment of our throat chakra, and our expression becomes the communion of one spirit, one mind, one heart. The sexual act has brought the two into one, and duality merges into unity. Ultimately, there is no awareness of two egos joined together but rather of one consciousness. The Tao of relationship is experienced as bliss, ecstasy, and rapture. The two beings are no longer separate from each other or separate from God/dess. This unity consciousness becomes truly real and the symbol for our new life.

Healing Sexual Addiction: The Case of Ted

Since the sexual energy is so deep and fundamental to being human, it usually holds important issues for us. These issues are based in past lives (or in the collective unconsciousness of the past). Blockages within the sexual energy are always blockages to communication. So as we become conscious of our sexual energy, a major realm of potential relationship opens to us.

Recently I worked with a handsome, forty-year-old "corporate scientist," Ted, who came to work on sexual addiction. His family upbringing consisted of a distant father and a dominant mother, both of whom rarely demonstrated any physical affection or intimate emotional behavior. A strong family codependancy developed in the family, where Ted, being the youngest of three children, felt a deep separation and aloneness while growing up. Love was something that had to be won; failing to win, a judgment was created and internalized, resulting in an irrational feeling of unworthiness —"I'm not worthy of love"—but his search for it continued.

Ted married at the beginning of his Saturn Return (twenty-eight years old) but an agreement was made to keep it open; both partners were permitted to have sexual relations with others. For Ted, sex became a means to an end, but the means quickly became a "demon" that possessed him and prevented him from fulfilling his real desire for love. His addiction now controlled his life, and his karmic issues grew into intense reminders of his inability to find happiness and peace.

An addiction taunts us by giving us a fleeting taste of happiness, but then it requires more and more in order to reach the moment of satiation. The sexual act has all the ingredients of an unavoidable intoxicant. The need for sex is rooted in our survival instinct. When this primordial energy is combined with fear and vulnerability, the mixture may imprint the ecstasy of orgasm with layers of emotional pain. This pain may arise from separation anxiety after sexual union or from falling out of love, or from the subtle yet powerful "coming down" after the sexual act. Thus the seeds are immediately sown to repeat the karmic act one more time as we attempt to return to a state of pleasure.

Ted was intellectually very aware of this repetition—his past years of therapy attested to that—but this intellectual understanding did little more than show him the prison he was in; it did not energetically release him from his bondage.

Ted's First Session

In Ted's first session, his first experience was of his family.

Ted: *A lot of laughter in the family—there are games among the family members to make light of things, of the serious things, to make a joke of them. I feel compelled to participate, but my mother, who is stern and hard to please, makes me feel separated. I feel fear. She reacts with superficial lovingness, but she's detached....*

I see that she's terribly afraid and angry. If she loves, she feels that she will be hurt; if she's dependent, she'll be hurt. I feel separated.

I want to say that she should be open and loving because there can be no pain or hurt in that; only good can come from loving. From that it will transmute and she will go beyond her hurt and pain, but she doesn't believe me. She feels safe in her pain and hurt. Control comes of it, the safety from the control—I feel confused. I try to love her, to be open with her.

I feel good in the loving, but something doesn't feel right in not having a receptor. My mind says it shouldn't make a difference, but I know it does, it takes energy from me. I feel the difference between casting my love, if it is love, to a nonreceptor and to casting it to a receptor like Jon (his last lover); one is draining, and the other is energizing. This makes me not want to love my mother. It seems futile. It doesn't make a difference. I feel sad and angry—sad that she doesn't return my love, yet I know that she loves me, but....

I'm in the womb; I'm a baby in my mother's womb. I don't think she wants me. She's angry, she feels discomfort. She's very busy trying to be a housewife, trying to be comfortable. She just puts up that superficial facade and tries to put things in place, but they won't stay in place. She tries to find happiness, but it eludes her; it slips away. There's no love in her life. This baby is a disruption; she didn't want to have another baby, and I feel that. I feel separated, like I don't belong, that I'm an intrusion.

(Ted moves forward to the moment of his birth.)

I feel so alone. I see a lot of bright light, a piercing light. There are feelings of confusion of what to do. The same separation is there, but I feel it in a different way. Now the symbols are changing—hieroglyphics, in a background of orange. It feels like a preparation, but I feel subservient to it, and there's a contraction in my body. I'm confined for some reason, confined to learn something. I can't get to the message until I work through the confinement or go beyond it.

Mother was a teacher to me previously. I'm standing in front of this wall of hieroglyphics and there is a figure there— half human and half animal. It has an animal head and a white robe. It is pointing at the wall. I don't understand. It does have a love and beauty and a sense of wisdom.

I'm hearing a message of the healing power of love—it's coming from my Higher Self. It's a deer, and it's full of love and wisdom. I connect....

I'm feeling the separation of physical love versus spiritual love. My Higher Self shows me that physical love is ephemeral and may be a distraction to me. It's been a mirror, a challenge for me to overcome. Unless I understand and overcome it, I won't get to the center of my spiritual love. I need to find a way to express my physical love without sacrificing my spiritual growth and my movement toward spiritual love. I have a strong attachment to the physical.

Now I see the symbol of my Higher Self, the deer; it lays down in the soft grass. It is saying to come back to myself, to be by myself....

(End of session.)

Session one focuses on Mother as the mirror of Ted's relationship issues, especially dealing with intimate and loving behavior. Since his mother represents "woman," her behaviors of separation—being hard to please and seemingly incapable of finding happiness—set the stage for Ted to play out his dramas of codependancy and addiction in relationship, especially with women.

Since it is common to internalize another's suffering—or we could say that we attract a person who mirrors our own karmic issues—Ted has created a situation to help him look at the following issues:

- a woman who is hard to please
- separation, detachment, not belonging, aloneness
- superficiality
- fear, anger, sadness, pain—the illusion of safety in these familiar energies
- safety by controlling
- needing a receptor for love, or else feeling drained
- the futility of loving mother/woman

- not being wanted by mother/woman
- inability to find happiness
- separation of physical and spiritual love
- attachment to the physical
- not understanding

The Higher Self brings the illumination of consciousness to Ted's numerous issues. It provides him the clarity to view these old energies and see their relationship to his sexual addiction and his difficulty in communicating with mother/woman. His last sentence sets the stage for healing: "Higher Self is saying to come back to myself." By coming back to Self, Ted can empower himself with his true spirit and thereby energetically shed the attachments and illusions that have blocked his heart from love and communion with another.

Ted's Second Session

The second session takes Ted into a past-life experience as an illegitimate child whose father, a king, orders that the child be taken from his commoner mother and be abandoned in the forest. The child feels the separation from people; many pass him by because they are aware of who he is and fear the wrath of the king. The child feels their fear and doesn't understand. He feels himself to be an innocent victim and is angry that they don't accept him. He also feels hurt and alone.

His mother finally discovers the whereabouts of her child and sends a man to rescue him from the forest. The child feels tremendous relief, love, and security in the man's arms since the man loves the child as his own.

Ted exclaims, "I feel happy to have someone to love me. He has such a great love. He brings me to my mother, but she's very bitter. I'm confused about my mother's bitterness, the love of this man (Jon), and the separation from my father."

The child's mother is in a rage. She feels the pain of what the king has done with their child and wants revenge to purge her anger. This vow is held within. Time passes.

The boy grows up to be a warrior but doesn't feel comfortable in the act of killing: he sees it only as effective in maintaining order. There comes a great rebellion, and his friend and mentor (Jon) and father, the king, are both killed. Ted becomes very angry and bitter about his loss and rises to become the ruler. This is not comfortable for him because he finds that he must act from viciousness in order to maintain his rule. He watches as his armies invade the peace of nature and converge on a defenseless village, slaughtering all—even women and children.

"There is no feeling for the people," says Ted. "I watch from a distance, separated from what's happening, though I have created this incident. I have sent them out to destroy, to bring fear to the people so that they will obey me. Some of the women are brought back to be used for the men's pleasures. I feel a tightness in my chest, a deep tension."

After the deaths of Jon and his father, Ted falls victim to his accumulated guilt. "I have become just like my father," he says. "There is no escape. I can't change it. I don't care anymore. Things are falling apart, a decadence in the land. It's very ugly."

"I feel a lance piercing through my abdomen. It is held by my mother. She sees me as my father was, as insane as my father. She kills me as him. I feel very sad; I've made a mistake in not being strong enough to do what was right. I had the chance to change things, but I let it slip away. I deserve to die; I certainly don't deserve to rule over anyone else."

"My Higher Self appears as a powerful lion," Ted continues. "And my mother is talking to the lion. The lion walks over to my body and pulls the lance out and carries me to the woods. I stay there and decompose as I watch. It feels nice."

"There is some relationship between Jon and the lion. Jon tried to raise me with the capability of being different, but I chose differently. Why? I was separated from my truth. The separation made it possible for something else to take hold of me. There is important work to do on releasing my separation, integrating my truth, and feeling the unity that can keep my truth close to me."

When Ted is asked who the mother and father in the story represent in his life today, he immediately answers, "My father then was my father in this lifetime and my mother who killed me is my ex-wife, Joan."

(End of session.)

This session takes Ted back to see what happened in a previous lifetime in order to understand his present predicament. The themes of separation are clearly demonstrated. Ted is separated from his mother and other people as the result of judgment, and he is separated from his loved ones because of war and rebellion. *Separation leads to judgment, which leads into guilt.* We see further the embodiment of another person's emotional energies, this time from the father. Ted's guilt calls in the need for punishment. The symbolically sexual lance brings death with Ted's statement of self-judgment: "I deserve to die."

In this scenario, the role of women is filled with the energies of separation/judgment. Most importantly, it is the mother/woman energy that imprints Ted with the murder. His emotional body holds this memory from that point forward, and the presence of a woman will trigger the karmic pain of that imprint. Only Jon, a man, is permitted to give Ted love. In both sessions, we see the basis of Ted's suffering as *the absence of the unifying force of love* engendered by the fundamental karma of separation/judgment.

Ted's Third Session

Session 3 began with the Higher Self taking the symbolic form of a snake.

Ted: *I see images of being used sexually. I feel so alone; I'm being used as punishment. I'm in a male body; I'm in my 20's. It is some early time period. They use me to impregnate women; it's some kind of punishment for not wanting to kill as a warrior. I feel so used. There's no love, and I want love, but we are not allowed to love. The women are afraid of me. A ruling woman controls it all. She is punishing me for not doing something. I am a warrior, a defensive warrior; we protect our people. We don't take an aggressive stand. She wants me to kill or hurt someone, to be destructive, and I won't do it. I refuse to go on the offense in her war. I feel sorry for the people, sorry for myself.*

She makes me impregnate women. Then later she wants me to impregnate her; she wants to have a child with me. I won't do it. I really don't like her. I'm being threatened with death if I don't do it. I'm filled with anger, but strangely, I also feel love. It's confusing. It's a horrible situation. I just want to die, but I don't choose death. I feel caught, and as a result, I feel like a coward. I go to her; there are snakes all around her. She gives me some kind of drug in a drink. It makes me feel different. I feel great power, some dizziness, and detachment, but also a screaming in my head, a fear inside. I try to make love with this woman but it feels wrong. I can't come to orgasm. The frustration is making me rageful. I want to kill this person. I know that I'm committing a great sin. I feel this raging battle within me. Inside I ask for help; I ask God to save me.

Then I feel the orgasm—a great release but something is wrong. I see white light everywhere and a great love, but there is a great pain in my left side and back.

She stabbed me! I didn't feel it at first because of the orgasm but when I came inside her, she stabbed me with a knife. Then I felt her hatred, but also love from her. I feel love for her. It's so confusing. I'm dead, but not dead.... I'm joining with the snake. I see the woman is Joan" (his ex-wife from the present lifetime).

After some time of silence Ted's Higher Self talked to him about his sexual habits and his attitudes about sex. His Higher Self showed him how he feels defeated by his addiction and how he feels helpless to change his life. At the same time he felt a strong pain in his chest running down into his groin. His Higher Self helped him clear the energy and he came back to peace in his heart.

Ted: *I see the woman* (Joan) *in a background of gold light. She's holding a beautiful wand; it has a bright pink iridescence around it. Joan hands it to me and says it's mine, that I had lost it, and now I will need it. I need to use it for spiritual healing. I use it on my body, and I feel a clearing, a releasing of my pain, my age-old burdens. I feel clear.*

(End of session)

The imprinting of sex as punishment, as humiliating, as devoid of love and intimacy are powerful energetic memories to carry around in our auric field. They are subtly communicated to our partner. They are a constant source of frustration.

Ted felt he must fight, control, or release through orgasm this frustration. Now he sees clearly the imprint of death that has been associated with orgasm—how every future orgasm will trigger that familiar rush of emotion, complete with the memory of death. Feelings of the release, the woman's hatred, a moment of love, and the pain of the stabbing (in the kidney, the source of sexual energy) are all a confused jumble that create the emotional memory. With imprints like this, it is clear how potent issues can block the love of sexual union.

Fortunately, the Higher Self, having released the memories of the past through the power of consciousness, provides advice and guidance about Ted's sexual habits and attitudes, and then brings forth the energy of the Divine Woman. Symbolized by his ex-wife, she offers him a symbolic sexual tool of transformation to use to release "age-old burdens." The use of the energetic tool and the imprinting of the positive archetypal energy of the Divine Woman replaces the old, negative, addictive patterns within Ted's emotional body. This opens him to new possibilities of relationship based in consciousness and the fulfillment of the need for love.

Yin is the mediator between the yang and the transcendentally Divine. When yin is rejected or denied, a failure of communication occurs and the yang, now unbalanced from its complement, can no longer act from unity. Being separate, judgement occurs to extend and perpetuate the separation between the superficial aspects of materiality and the subtle realms of the Divine.

This phenomenon has been seen in our perceptions and judgments toward sexuality. The control and victimization of the feminine (yin) by the negative (perverse) masculine (yang) is the story of history over the last 3,000 years since the overthrow of the Goddess by phallocracy. The subsequent development of the schism that created profane ideas of sexuality is a result of a male dominated judgment concept that we still cling to today.

A Session with Linda

The following session of Linda's touches the themes of our infamous history, the fall of Eden, the fall of the consecration of spiritual sexuality. The victimization of the feminine principle is archetypal and a constant reminder of our present predicament on this planet. The separation of the yin and yang due to the expansion of masculine-motivated judgmental belief still surrounds us today. This powerful session gives us hope, as it reminds us of our fall from grace and our healing into unity.

Personally, Linda (age 30) experienced rape at 17 and the imprint of that violation resisted years of therapy. She has suffered both emotionally and physically with genital herpes since the time of the rape.

Linda: *I see myself as a young woman, innocent yet aware, full of light that radiates through me as a grace. Love is what I know, what I am. I'm in a simple, but beautiful temple overlooking water—maybe on an island in the Mediterranean Sea. I must be a priestess; this temple feels like home, it's where my function lies, my purpose in this life. I serve the temple and by doing so, I serve the people. The temple is the home of the Goddess, she is my source, she fills me with the light of Love and Healing for the people. I love her so.... My life is dedicated to her expression and through that I feel such grace and beauty, such a warm caring for her creation, her children—my children. I have been taught her wisdom through the inner light she blesses me with, and through the sacred body that she infuses me with. I have become her physical connection to the people; when she inhabits me with her loving being I can help men and women connect to their source, the Divine energy that is so full of love.*

I see this connection with the people as mostly sexual; whether it be man or woman, the sexual act is one of spiritual union, an opening to another reality where the masculine and feminine become one, where the ego dissolves into a unity of love, where the Goddess and the God celebrate creation, where basic forces ignite new life, and new possibilities of creativity. This love balances that which is out of balance, harmonizes the disharmonies within the psyche, heals the pain of too much separation. I can help by opening myself to the power of the Divine and receiving the person into me, into the now Divine consort. Even women can be received; physical anatomy is not a limitation, because we are both male and female, and the maleness is received and nourished by the Goddess without discrimination; love unifies without prejudice. The temple is only a locus for Divine interaction; it is my training and my blessing of this experience that has allowed me to play this role for others. I was taught and I will teach and others will follow and the opportunity will spread to those in need of the sacred.

Facilitator: What happens to you as you get older?

Linda: *For many years I play this role within the temple, and for many years there is peace in the land. But...* (Tears)

Facilitator: What's happening?

Linda: *But something happens. It does not last. There is a new government. Strangers from the North, men without heart. Men who use their phallus as a weapon, men who reject the Goddess, who profane our rituals of love. They treat us as prostitutes, they use our bodies with violence and selfish desire, they treat us with such disgrace and profanity. This was unknown until they came, an insult to the Goddess.*

(Tears)
And then the tragedy occurred. (Tears)

Facilitator: What was the tragedy?

Linda: *The Goddess left. She no longer came to me and others. She was annihilated by the violence; the rape of our hearts and our bodies created a barrier to the opening of the Divine. We felt like victims; the safety of our hearts was destroyed; all we knew was sexual abuse instead of sexual liberation. Pain overshadowed ecstasy; the penis sent waves of fear through our bodies, and the body became hard and cold; no life, no celebration, no joy was left in us. Without the Goddess we became dead to each other, separate from each other. The vicious masculine created a rift in our unity with the Divine, it separated the life force from our conscious lives, it divorced us from our source. And what happened as a result is that the acts of love embodied in our sexual spirituality were replaced by the darkness of judgments. The acts became profane, controlled by a dominating rule. Sexuality became tainted, women were property, objects of desire and controlled as a result. The masculine ruled with a closed heart.*

Facilitator: What happened to you?

Linda: *I became infected with a venereal disease. Through the violence I was infected as I was forced to have sex. I was raped, victimized; I spread the infection. I, among many, died as a result. I still hold this memory within me today.*

Facilitator: Ask the Goddess to come to you now. Ask her to help you.

Linda: *Yes, I feel her now. I feel her soft, warm love embracing*

*my body and infusing me as she did so long before. I feel the
tears running down my cheeks; I have missed her so, so much.
I felt so lost, so abandoned for so long. Goddess clears the
memories of hate and abuse. She releases the disease of hate,
the memory I've carried and suffered with for so long. Now I
can realign the sexual energy with the spiritual light. Finally
I can return to the sacred sexuality, to that radiance of the
Divine magic that has the power to create life without the
blinding feeling of pain.*

Facilitator: Ask her to heal your body.

Linda: *The Goddess clears the memories of hate and abuse.
She releases the disease of hate, the memory I've carried and
suffered with for so long. Now I can realign the sexual energy
with the spiritual light. Finally I can return to the sacred
sexuality, to that radiance of the Divine magic that has the
power to create life without the blinding feeling of pain. I'm
home again; I feel the temple around me, we are one again. I
am so grateful.*
(End of session)

Sexual Ecstasy: The Case of Lin

Most of the time, clients come to the Deva Foundation
because there is a problem or unresolved issue that needs
work. With this intention, deep shadow work is usually the
result. But, of course, if a client changes the intention, then it
is possible to move into a different type of experience.

Lin arrived at Deva with the need to explore sexual unity,
with the intention of imprinting both a new approach in his
sexual relationship with his wife, Sandi, and to expand his

connection with the Divine. After one session of energetic clearing of sexuality and judgment themes, Lin's second session exceeded his wildest dreams.

A Session with Lin

Facilitator:　Ask your Higher Self to take you into an experience of sexual relationship that you need at this time. Speak out the first image or feeling that comes.

Lin: *My Higher Self appears as an indigenous man, middle aged, dressed in a loincloth with different-colored paints on his body. He appears like a shaman and his energy is incredible; he's radiating white light from his heart that glows all around him like an aura.*

Facilitator:　Connect with that energy. Draw it into your body, take it through yourself, into every cell.

Lin: *I feel that powerful energy pouring through me. It awakens me.*

He's taking me into a mountain forest—beautiful tall ponderosa pines, red rocks, unbounded views across a vast expanse. We come to a cave in the mountain and we go inside. It is cooler, damp but somehow there is a soft light filling the cave; it seems to come from a hole above.

I ask my Higher Self what this place is and why we have come here. He just smiles and remains quiet. He motions to a flat place to sit; it's covered in a soft moss. We sit, and he closes his eyes. I follow the gesture and notice my breathing is slowing down, becoming softer.

My body on the massage table is quite still; I feel really deep. I'm going into a transcendental state of consciousness. It's very similar to meditation, but somehow different—maybe because I'm talking to you and at the same time feeling the profound depth.

Facilitator: Just be in the silence and see what happens. Let your Higher Self guide you.

Lin: *I feel his energy all around me, as if it is activating or enlivening this space, this shared consciousness. He says, "Are you ready for a sex lesson?"*

Tarzan here has a sense of humor! I say, "Sure!"

Then he says, "Dear Earth Goddess, the teacher of life in this dimension, the knower of love and relationship, grace us with your presence."

At first I feel a thrill through my body, and then I notice Tarzan disappears into brilliant white light and I'm left alone in the cave. But there is certainly a presence of love, a comfort here, even though I feel a bit expectant. So I come back to my breath and feel the energy building in me.

Suddenly there is a wave of energy through my body and simultaneously I become aware of a feminine presence. She's not clear. Wait a minute....

It's a dark woman with jet-black hair. She's so big—I mean large—and so full of energy— large, full breasts, quite voluptuous. I can feel the sexual energy react within me. I realize that I am naked, that she's naked, and I immediately feel self-conscious. She notices my subtle shift of embarrassment and says, "What is this uneasy feeling? Does your nakedness bother you? Are you willing to open your awareness to it?"

Instantly I feel my attention moving into the uneasy feeling, and just as instantly I see, multidimensionally, its source. This is amazing. I've never had such a sense of clarity, of knowing.

Then, I feel a wave of sadness. We live with so much judgment and so much shame. I feel it in the body, this incredible creation of yours (of the Goddess). It's as if we really did buy this sales pitch of Christianity. This horrendous idea of original sin! And we took it into our bodies; we literally imprinted this shame physically, so that we're flawed, not good enough, never good enough.... (Tears)

I'm ashamed of my body, ashamed to be human, to be this emotional, sexual being. I really bought it! I see how my nakedness symbolizes how I see my true self. I'm shameful, that's who I am. Exposed for what I really am, and that feels embarrassing, shameful, guilty of some unknown crime of being.... (More tears)

Now I see how my life, my parents, my schools, and every aspect of my society lays this sin of sex on me. It's a wonder we ever procreate. Wouldn't that be the cosmic joke! Through our social sexual programming we extinguished the species, as if we forgot to "be fruitful and multiply." How did they expect us to do that without sex?

I know this doesn't make sense, but I'm really angry. There are just too many rules and regulations. "This is good; this is bad; this is right only when you do this and this. That shame hurts so bad. My poor body holds such pain. Imagine, to be naked and feel the pain. I also realize how this nakedness makes me so vulnerable and now so open to more hurt, more rejection.

Facilitator: Move into this rejection.

Lin: *Well, if I'm not worthy, being essentially flawed, then how could I be loved. And accepted, especially by you?*

The Goddess says, "Come here my love. Let me hold you. Let me show you your physical perfection."

I move into her arms and feel such heat, such softness. She strokes me, and I feel waves of energy penetrating into my body, releasing the pain.

She says, "Let it go. Let it all go. Now. You keep me away with all this shame; it's just not real. I don't judge you, so don't judge yourself. You have a divine body, just like every creation of Spirit. Are you willing to let it go?"

Yes, absolutely! She holds me tighter. Her love is just unbelievable. You can only surrender. There's no resistance that blocks that quality of love.... (Tears)

Then she changes form. She has turned into a young deer. Soft, gentle, and so tender and sweet. Then into a dolphin. Such a joy, a passion for life. I see her playing in the waves like a dance. Now she switches to a long iridescent snake, not a scary one but a happy snake, She's moving across the cave floor with such a sensual grace. She comes up my thigh and coils around my leg, such a warmth and strength. I feel energy moving.

Oh, my God! She's coiling around my penis; its so intense. I am so erect, and she keeps squeezing me, a pulsation; my penis just seems to grow. She just keeps coiling, now up across my torso to my heart. Her tongue flickering on my heart chakra.

I close my eyes tightly and feel the sexual power; the infinite strength coursing through my body; it's so big.

Then I hear her voice: "Does this feel better?" Her voice is pure sensation. It makes my skin tingle. "Yes? A little better than shame?" I can't believe this is happening to me. The waves are so intense.

She turns back into her human form and rubs against me; her breasts opening me even wider. Her pubic hair is like a soft brush across my stomach. She rises up, her huge breasts caress my mouth, and I realize I'm making love with the Goddess. My body is wide open and ready, my feeling is nothing but love, but a love I've never experienced before. It's strong, empowered, it has the life force in it. My mind is hyper-alert, totally awake. I don't feel out of control, though I guess I expected to be overwhelmed by all of it. I feel totally centered and totally excited.

Her voice, "Open your heart. Open your energy to me. Give of yourself. Come love me."

(Lin's body undulates—passionate, sensual, and powerful. He whispers, he cries. The sexual act continues, full-blown for about 25 minutes)

Facilitator: What's happening?

Lin: *I was creating love. It's the only way I can describe it. The creation of love, of Spirit, that which is truly divine. Through the creation of this infinite power of love, I felt my body transform into a vessel of love and light. Sex on this level creates not just the miracle of a child, but the preliminary energy, or thoughtform that can manifest a soul. It's so incredibly beautiful!*

My body became pure light. Each orgasm—there must have been millions—was a new creation of love. Each one brought me a little closer, a little more integrated with her. It was the first time I ever had orgasms without ejaculating.

The Goddess became all women, the pure yin principle. She was nothing but sensuality, tenderness, playfulness; she is the uninhibited playmate, just reveling in the partnership. And of course, a radiance of nonjudgment. That is the great gift. To be with a woman who is free of any judgment, no barrier, just unconditional love. Sex is infused with its deepest value of joining, just being one. We were one—the words seem so inadequate to describe an experience where there are two beings fitting inside of each other on an essential level. This space is perfectly integrated, where there is no difference, no

*separation, where you can just flow in the thrill of it all.... What
a gift!* (Laughing)

*The Goddess asks if I think we could market this. Why does
my Higher Self have such a strange sense of humor?*

*She says I now know the Kundalini energy and I will never
forget it. That knowing is imprinted and available always as
a healing and nourishing flow.*

*She says this is only the beginning—and to remember that
all this experience, all this love is within me, and it always will
be.*

(End of session)

The question arises, "Is this just a sexual fantasy, or does
it have practical therapeutic effect?" If you ask Lin this
question, you will hear him say, "It changed my life." He
claims that it gave him a new perspective of what sex, love,
and intimate relationship are all about. Clearing the old habits
and creating a new and healthier sexual response is what this
type of personal transformation produces.

From a spiritual point of view, the Goddess may be a
spiritual being who has come to teach and support Lin's
healing, or she may be Lin's creation, symbolically manifest-
ing to give him permission to open himself to his sexual beauty
and passion. Seen through the lens of the spiritual, Lin can
associate his instinctual sexual feelings with the evolutionary
need for unity, not only with a loved one but with Spirit. This
new connection will have the effect of quickening the sexual
vibration within him, which will energetically nourish all
aspects of his being. The heart and kidney energy rejuvenate
as a result. And his auric field will touch others with his new-
found loving light.

5

∞

Communicating with Spirit

Pure consciousness is that nonlocal, intelligent, omnipresent field that lies at the basis of all creation. It is the fabric of connectiveness, the medium of communication between one individual and another, and between the past, the present, and the future, regardless of apparent limitations of space-time. The field of consciousness is a field of infinite communication possibilities.

The Field of Consciousness

It is written in the esoteric literature throughout the ages that all psychic phenomena arise from the ability to tap into the nonlocal qualities of consciousness and use this *field of all possibilities* as the source for creation and manifestation. On that transcendental level, all is connected. The doors are open multidimensionally. Thoughts, feelings, the past, the present, and the future are all available to one's awareness. The ability to create, transmit, or alter matter, energy—even reality—is possible from the subtlest levels of the relative world to the surface levels of life. (Within any psychic phenomenon, whether it be *clairvoyance, clairaudience,* or tuning into another's thoughts or feelings, the field of pure consciousness is utilized.)

Far-sensing, which includes clairvoyance and clairaudience (the ability to see or hear at a distance), becomes possible if *space* is no longer a limit. And the abilities to know events of the past, present, or future, such as premonition, precognition, or prophecy, become possible if *time* is no longer a limit. If our mind, in the sense of its ability to think and feel, is also nonlocal, then our consciousness can join with another's mind and experience his or her thoughts, feelings, and desires. Being joined, it becomes natural to telepathically communicate thoughts and/or energy to another, regardless of distance.

The reality of an omnipresent field as the fundamental ground state of communication opens up all possibilities to us. "All possibilities" is actually a characteristic of consciousness. Pure consciousness is a field of infinite potential. It is the unmanifest source from which all creation springs. All configurations of matter and energy arise from it, structuring creation. By transcending the relative world of form and experiencing the pure consciousness within, we open to our ability to literally do anything, create anything, know anything. *All psychic abilities manifest from the omnipresent field of pure consciousness.*

If these psychic, mental, and physical abilities are so empowering to the human species, why have we not seen more evidence of natural selection for these qualities? Psychic and mental powers seem to offer us advantages in survival and the ability to overcome suffering and illness, so why do relatively few people exhibit these talents? And if one does have a particular gift, such as psychokinesis, why aren't other abilities also present? And why is it so difficult to develop them?

One theory is that our social environment may limit the expression of psychic abilities; that is, we keep such experiences to ourself for fear of judgment. Many within the general public either deny their personal experiences or keep them private. In traditional native cultures, there is often a framework for expressing these abilities. There may be more psychic development and an openness that is generally lacking in Western, scientific-oriented societies. The Western mind, having no objective model for understanding such things, has projected its own ignorance and misunderstanding on indigenous shamanistic cultures by judging them as superstitious and ignorant, as if to say, "If your shamanism doesn't fit into our scientific paradigm it must not be real. So, let us educate you in our truth." This patronizing attitude of science has caused a degeneration and tragic loss of shamanistic culture, including the invaluable understanding of the inner worlds. The psychic abilities and sacred technologies exemplified in thousands of years of shamanistic practice provide the database for researching and validating psychic phenomena. Even though a growing number of parapsychological researchers are attempting to develop both technical and theoretical models for psychic phenomena, our relatively new scientific culture has not found satisfactory models of reality or even successful hypotheses to understand the inner dimensions.

Also, there is the influence of religion and modern attitudes: psychic phenomena are judged harshly and associated with belief systems that many people fear. This, combined with addictions to superficial materialism, keeps psychic phenomena and subtle energetics from developing as a natural part of who we are.

Another explanation, although esoteric, is quite common and evident in psychospiritual therapy. One of the core themes that many spiritual seekers are attempting to heal is the masculine issue of the abuse of power. This negative yang energy wants to control—usually through violence and aggression.

Power is one of the great seducers. It weaves a web that entraps. There is the victimizer's addiction to the "rush" of power; there is the addiction to being the victim of another's power; and there is just being the *victim* to the addiction. It can be overshadowing, diminishing our abilities. Power is the manifestation of energy to do work. How we use power is our test; and the effect it has on us is part of that test.

In Deva sessions, the Higher Self often takes a client's consciousness into karmic memories where there was a misuse of power that has left a deep imprint. As a result of separation, this imprint creates in the victim's and victimizer's consciousness harsh judgments. The emotional chain reaction of the separation/judgment theme usually brings a person to a demand for punishment, which may include the promise that power will never be abused again. Unfortunately, *fear of power* is often part of the karmic theme, so any ability or behavior that expresses power is shut down or tightly controlled out of fear of repetition.

Since consciousness is the source of all manifestation, its potential power is unlimited. The spiritual masters of the past knew of the power of consciousness and the temptation to misuse it. They offered their teachings only to those who were prepared and wise enough to handle the responsibility. Even so, abuse of spiritual power existed and is still experienced today. Fortunately, the abuse of consciousness does not destroy consciousness (though in its extreme, it could destroy manifest creation, part and parcel). But experience teaches us that when a karmic lesson is learned, we are less likely to repeat it. At the same time, others are influenced by the "resonance" of this newly found wisdom and the collective wisdom expands.

The abuse of power has been a theme in this world for eons. The consequences have grown exponentially to the point that we human beings now have the ability to destroy the planet. If this continues, our negative potential may expand out beyond the solar system. If the abuse of power is drawn inward into deep energetic realms of creation, there is no telling what destruction of subtle realms might be possible.

But inherent within consciousness is the ability to create, to heal, and to balance the extremes of polarity. Like a pendulum that swings to one extreme, we may see that it can swing to the other, continuing to swing back and forth. We may then realize that we need not play this game anymore, and the pendulum of life's polarities stop. We transcend into unity consciousness, free of duality. The following is an example of that process/possibility.

An Abuse-of-Power Session

Sydney: *My vision expands beyond this earth into the cosmos. I see the galactic consciousness; I am this immensity, so expanded, so powerful.*

I am a galactic being, not of human form but of some kind of immense light-body consciousness. I know how to create and how to dissolve my creation. It is just a matter of thought and desire. I communicate with other beings like myself.... But, something feels uncomfortable.

Facilitator: Go into it. What is the feeling?

Sydney: *There is some sort of arrogance or distorted self-satisfaction—or maybe a self-righteousness—to this being....*

I see him talking, communicating with these others as if they're gods deciding the future of their subordinates—in essence, passing judgment. Now it looks like Earth, and its inhabitants are the playthings of these so-called "gods."

Facilitator: What do you do? What happens?

Sydney: *I descend onto Earth in the form of a man. I still have* *my powers, my awareness of my status. There's such arrogance. I feel I must change things and clean things up—these humans are so stupid! They don't know how to live. Such ignorance— I must purge this ignorance and decadence.* (Breathing increases.)

Time has no limit. I create a massive volcanic eruption. It spreads a layer of ash through the atmosphere. It darkens the sky, the sun, the moon. It sends panic into the hearts of men. They know it's an omen of punishment. The climate changes— storms, floods, droughts, insects ravish crops, people die. It's the purge.

In another time, I create the plague—epidemics of disease. It kills more. Few survive. The body disintegrates. The fear is alive.

I create a world of fire, an explosion of killing light. It destroys the world. I purge by light, by fire, to purify, yet the fear remains. It's a hell fire to purge their ignorance. There is no other way; the earth must begin again. Their drug of ignorance keeps them suffering. The people fight each other; they even kill their families. They can't even talk to each other. It's like a world of total aloneness. Everybody is in their own prison. The doors are locked tightly.... (Tears)

I must purge them of their judgment by being their judgment! I am their consciousness of aloneness and separation.

Wait a minute. (Pause for five minutes)

Such power! I am the god of their creation. I am the manifestation of their arrogance, of their misuse of life, power, all their misuse. Just as I can create and destroy, humanity creates and destroys. They created the cloud of ash from the volcano. They created the darkness that blocked the energy of their spirit-sun. They created the plague, the nuclear storm. My God!

It's not about the past only, it's now, the volcanoes, the air pollution from our cars, our industries, our pain. It's AIDS, starvation, nuclear contamination, toxic waste. It is truly the ignorance. *We are in prisons of suffering....* (Tears)

I am the god of misuse of galactic power. I am that energy which maintains the gap between people, that won't allow the prison doors to open so we can listen to each other. The thickness of ignorance is like a wall to the psychic touch of our common divinity and inter-connectedness.

I am also the god of their guilt. I remember the time before we retreated behind the veil of illusion; before ignorance shut down our unbounded awareness. I remember when we could talk without words, hear without sound, see without eyes; when spirit was the mode of communication; when the senses were spiritual rather than so limited physically. Spirit was the pathway, common to all, the connection that made us one. But our judgment shut it all down. We imprisoned ourselves in denial—in the grand ignorance, no longer wanting to see. We panicked. The form took over, the body disconnected us from Spirit. But it was the guilt that we had failed. The misuse of our power took us into its grip. Suffering was our punishment. We thought suffering was our punishment from a higher power. The guilt created the victim; we just perpetuated it—we created a god to continue doing it to us.

I am the god they created, the destroyer....

I am so tired of it all. Yet there are some who see the illusion of it all, some who are not deluded, some who know. Their reality is not one of the prison; they create a different reality: one of love, of healing. They are the healers of this ignorance.

Yes, I see it now. I can be their god of healing, of lessons learned, their god of wisdom. Just as I manifested the world's need for suffering, I can now manifest the world's need for transformation.

I clear the darkness that obscured the light.
I heal the body of disease.

I neutralize the radiation of death.

I open the consciousness to the one, true God, the infinity of life.

As I open their consciousness, the ignorance simply disappears: no more illusion of separation, no more need to judge. And where there is no judgment, no guilt is felt, and no punishment, no victim, and no need to misuse life anymore. The crime of self-destruction is eradicated. I love creation... finally.

(End of Session)

This session exemplifies the ability to take responsibility for one's reality and to see that the inner mirrors the outer and vice versa. By opening the doors of his emotional body and taking the light of consciousness into his denial and illusions of ignorance, Sydney was able to see the core theme of abuse of power. Embodying that power, he became the god of power and witnessed his expression of it.

In Sydney's life before the session, he was aware of how his judgment manifested as a sharp tongue of criticism toward others, but mostly towards himself. He had an almost pathological need to "purge" his imperfections, to live a life of controlled purity—which of course, he could never accomplish. His judgment created more guilt, and the guilt created more punishment.

What is interesting is that until age ten, Sydney was extremely psychic, especially in the ability of psychokinesis. Then all his "powers" shutdown. For many years, this was a source of great frustration because he felt inside that he had done something wrong and was being punished.

Sydney's feeling after the session was that he now understood some of the reasons why he chose to shut down. We both agreed that this session should be interpreted symbolically, although some aspects of his experience have been played out in much the same way as he had seen them.

It was important for Sydney to allow his consciousness to penetrate into the painful memories in order to energetically clear any attachments of separation/judgment, abuse of power, and the resulting emotional suffering. Now comes the challenge of putting this information to work and allowing his potential to open up again. Having released his attachment to the addiction of power, Sydney may now be able to channel great power into his life without abusing it, his lesson learned.

Communicating With Spirit Through Spiritual Acupuncture

Communication with the spiritual realm of our being has been part of indigenous cultures since the beginnings of humanity. The methods of opening, connecting, and communicating with Spirit have always been enshrouded in the rich ceremonial life of people. The spiritual traditions, mythologies, and teachings of our enlightened ancestors provide symbolic "maps" and "practices" that help humanity live in accordance with natural law as well as to provide support for our evolution. These spiritual "technologies" are still available to us (although we may have lost our ability to understand and follow them correctly). In our own way, we can adapt and modify the old ways to suit us now, today.

Systems like massage, yoga, meditation, chanting, and dance have been part of human culture for thousands of years. We have been able to incorporate them into our life and as a result, we have seen great benefit.

One system I have been researching at the Deva Foundation with great success is the ancient system of spiritual acupuncture. In traditional Chinese medicine today, acupuncture and medicinal herbs are used mainly for the prevention and alleviation of illness. Acupuncture works well in many areas—especially problems with pain or other such manifestations of energy imbalance. Herbal medicine, many times used in conjunction with acupuncture, helps to restore the proper balance of yin and yang, allowing a person to adjust his or her body on an energetic level rather than on the superficial level of the symptom.

By working on deeper, more subtle levels of form, an approaching physical disease or disharmony can be alleviated prior to its tangible, symptomatic expression. This is the value of most forms of traditional medicine—they work energetically. Acupuncture is a good example because all that is necessary is to place thin needles in a few points, sometimes at a distance from the problem area, and relief or benefit arrives as if by magic. For example, maybe four needles are inserted in the extremities of the body for a person with an agonizing migraine headache. In fifteen minutes, with astonishment and relief, the person reports that the headache is gone! If we know how to work with energy, anything is possible.

At Deva, working with energy is the basis of our psychospiritual approach to holistic healing. We use a wide variety of techniques, but the power of consciousness is the foundation for all of them. As a practitioner of Traditional Chinese medicine, acupuncture has a special attraction for me. It's not the physical body application I find fascinating, but its use on the emotional and spiritual levels.

For at least two thousand years the Chinese have been treating people by stimulating known trigger points on the surface of the physical body. Needles, massage points (acupressure), and moxibustion (warming of acupuncture points with the herb mugwort) have been the main ways to manipulate the flow of *ch'i* (vital energy within the body). The science of acupuncture refined itself along with Chinese "shamanism" and other spiritual practices. The true masters integrated both the physical and the spiritual and saw how the treatment of the meridians combined with techniques of consciousness could work deeply on the level of Spirit. The clearing of emotional imprints, the expansion of consciousness, and the alleviation of physical symptoms combined to provide a truly holistic approach to healing. Spiritual work was integrated as part of one's life work. The Chinese doctor acted as a teacher, physician, and guide to facilitate healing and growth.

In Deva Work, the facilitator is not the guide (except to help the client connect with his or her own Higher Self or Inner Knowing); nor is the facilitator the physician—and seldom the teacher—since the client's experiences do the healing and teaching. The facilitator is merely a loving, nonjudgmental presence who encourages self-discovery. The client's intention sets the process in motion; and it is the client who does the work.

I have watched this process unfold beautifully and perfectly in more than three thousand sessions. Yet there are times when my Higher Self instructs me to use acupuncture to help the client more effectively open and clear energy that may be stuck or is in need of a little "push." When this happens, I carefully watch how the needles work and what they do to stimulate change.

The ancient masters used a set of acupuncture points, which they called *Windows of the Sky*, either alone or in conjunction with other points that stimulated a highly refined vibratory state of consciousness. These "spiritual" patterns of points freed consciousness to experience the multidimensional self and other spiritual realms of existence.

I have found these points quite effective in psychospiritual work whether exploring the expansion of consciousness, other realities, past lives, or ego transcendence. When used in conjunction with the *Window of the Sky* acupuncture points, the client can literally channel high-vibratory spiritual energy into an emotional imprint like anger, fear, or sadness; then quickly disengage that emotion and replace it with its spiritual counterpart such as peace or happiness.

When an organ or meridian is blocked, there are past karmic imprints or memories that are causing the blockage. We can move or dissipate the energy, temporarily, but then the emotion returns or lodges elsewhere, causing another occurrence, like a cancer that metastasizes. The channeling of spiritual energy, the energy of consciousness, *is* the energy of resolution, the true healing that changes us. As we let go of the blockage, the spiritual energy takes its place, transmuting bondage into freedom, ignorance into wisdom.

Window of the Sky acupuncture points promote transcendence. They are points of communication and communion. It is interesting that most of them lie around the throat chakra, the area of communication. These points take us beyond our judgment and separation and into higher realms of unity and Self. They help us to let go of ego constraints in order to rediscover who we *really* are. The true nature of reality becomes energetically a part of our awareness; Higher Self shines through us more clearly. The throat chakra unlocks the gates to the third eye. Realization dawns and enlightenment begins.

Once these spiritual points, whether "needled" or not, are activated, they energetically communicate as part of the natural function of transmutation and enlightenment. As they are activated, the karmic layers of separation fall away and the judgments, that have self-righteously flared our anger are released. Forgiveness then heals the sore spot in our emotional body, and we can come out of our separation to connect with love again.

It's interesting that the first point of the pericardium

meridian (of the heart) is a *Window of the Sky* point. This meridian's principal function is to protect the deeper heart energy. The *Window* points contribute to the expansion of consciousness and the release of ego attachment. The pericardium point helps the heart maintain its strength and sense of security. When the heart is secure in opening to pain or vulnerability, it becomes resilient in its ability to adapt—even to an experience of "heartbreak"—and fulfill its function of openhearted loving.

Another important *Window of the Sky* point is at the center of the throat chakra. It is one of the most symbolic and multidimensionally effective of all the points. If we can open this point, we can open the chakra to let stuck energies out or, if it is already cleared, to channel more powerful communication energies through it.

Most facilitators of psychospiritual work have their own methodologies for helping their clients to connect with Spirit. The ways and means are many, and the effectiveness of any given technique depends on many factors. In any case, consciousness *is* the ground state of our being, and it is the arena of *any* spiritual work. (The more we expand our consciousness and use it for communicating, the more effective will be our tools and techniques.)

Once we begin to open and utilize our infinite power of consciousness, we can begin to build a true foundation for all the possibilities of this world and others. Communicating with Spirit is the process of expanding our consciousness into an "altered state," where we may shift our awareness into a perspective that allows us to sense a new reality. The communication process remains essentially the same, although it is a different world, with different rules. By opening this new door of perception and taking a step into the subtler realms of creation, Spirit can be experienced from a new perspective. Each time we view the hologram of Spirit from a different angle, it draws us inward a bit more. Then we can know it more expansively until we realize it fully. Upon full recognition, we transcend the need for form and tangible experience, and we arrive at communion, where there is the unified experience of just being.

6

Breaking the Cycle of Separation
and Judgment

In the "beginning," we separate from the unity of God-consciousness as we come into form. Separation polarizes us into duality, and judgment comes into being. By its very existence within our consciousness, judgment perpetuates separation. The throat chakra controls this interplay by holding the karmic energy of separation/judgment, which in turn inhibits the throat chakra's communication function.

To be alive in a human body is a constant experience of separation. Being in a body, in this world of time and space, we view ourselves as separate, different from other beings, different from the trees, the clouds, the snow, the lizard—a different personality with a different way of seeing things. The theme of separation is an indulgence in which we are completely programmed to see ourselves as objects, forms that are different, and therefore separate from everything else. Given the power of separation, it takes skill to see unity, to see our connection with others and our environment.

Suffering accents our separation; the more suffering, the more we experience our separation. It's as if suffering were trying to teach us that separation is not the bliss of God; yet when the lesson of suffering is learned, it helps to bring us back to God. In those moments when we touch the bliss, we are touching unity, the true reality of oneness, of Universal Mind. Our karmic experiences would like us to believe otherwise, and unfortunately we often do. It seems that life is an ongoing schoolhouse in which the main subject of study is the theme of separation. To a great extent, each incarnation plays the same game under the same rules.

If we look at the progression of life, we start with a choice. Being in Spirit, outside of time and space, connected to the totality, we choose to incarnate. Whether it be a choice made on the basis of the collective, out of curiosity or from personal need, Spirit comes into form: beginning at conception, yin and yang come together to create body. The environment for this development is within the energy field of our mother; we are connected to her physically and energetically. We are undeveloped, barely physical. There is no intellect, no thought as to what is happening. What we do is *feel*. Our emotional body, created in past incarnations and imprinted with memory and karma, reaches out to sense through feelings. That which is immediate, Mother, becomes the primary focus of our attention, even though our consciousness still remembers the sense of unity we felt in the realm of the universal. As we develop, we continue to bridge the gap between our former unified reality and this, the relative world of duality. The gap between unity and form reminds us of our lifetimes of separation.

While we are in the womb, we are connected now physically and emotionally with Mother; we feel what Mother feels—her fear or joy, her pain or love. These feelings are the primary experiences of our evolving senses. After about nine months of growth in our mother's womb, the next step arrives—yet another experience of separation: we are released from the body, through physical birth and the cutting of the cord. Not only is the event itself traumatic but now we must breathe, eat, and function relatively independently of all other beings. As time passes, the experience of separation becomes even stronger and the memory of unity fades. At this stage, we hope to have bonded with our parents and still feel some connection.

If we have not bonded, then the separation is even more pronounced.

Our body grows and changes. Our senses develop and the dynamics of perception begin to create a reality of independent self. Our personality manifests, blending the repetitions of past karma with the present situation. Before we know it, we are lost again in the material world, programmed with who we *think* we are, what we *think* we should be doing, living the ancient theme of separation one more time. We see ourselves as members of the collective but we rebel in our individuality, demanding what we want from life. For many, life is a solo performance. Relationships come and go. Some are good, some are full of pain but nothing remains the same. Change is all we can depend on, so we hold on to what we can: memories, attitudes, familiar routines, anything that can ground us in what we feel is an unstable world. But as we grow old, to some extent, we realize the inevitability of death. We laugh to ourselves as we see that no one has ever failed at dying. Just as a beautiful maple tree drops its leaves each year as part of its cycle, we will drop this form. Nature has always been showing us how to let go, how to flow with the cycle of change in a world governed by time. Yet in ourselves and in others, we see the reluctance to let go of form, especially our emotionally structured memory with its habitual patterns of localized mind, and particularly the stuckness of the emotional body with its memory of pain and its fear of future pain. In a world where letting go is fundamental to the cycles of change, the harder we resist the greater the pressure of pain until we reach the threshold of death and are forced to surrender the need for control.

Our body *will* fall away, regardless of how hard we struggle. Let us watch nature to see how effortless letting go can be. When the time comes for death, another wonderful step in life has arrived: the opportunity to let go of our identification with form, to release separation and merge back into unity. Even though we drop our body and release our spirit from the third dimension, the transition may still be difficult. The physical body is only one aspect with which we have been identifying; dropping it does not imply that we drop the emotional body or mind body that is holding onto karmic memory. We carry these aspects of self with us into spirit, as we would carry baggage to our next destination. The karmic memory still impacts us as a separate form, and this can cause difficulty while in transition after death.

Separation/Judgment and the Tibetan Book of the Dead

The *Tibetan Book of the Dead* is a multidimensional treatise and guide for releasing the attachments of form and realizing unity. It helps us understand the "play" of our attachments, the struggle of the ego to maintain its integrity, and its need to continue to exist in identified, localized form. This ancient writing instructs us on how to let go and return to God.

The essence of the *Bardo Thodol* (Book of the Dead) teachings is that so long as the mind is identified with humanity, identified with the ego which is seen as individual and separate from other minds, it will be the "plaything" of *maya, of* ignorance. This influence causes us to look upon the mind's hallucinatory panorama of existence as real.

The theme of separation is intensely brought into focus in the mythical symbolism of Judgment Day, the moment when we must come face-to-face with our actions and the consequences of our life. Nothing of importance is allowed to be forgotten; all of it comes to consciousness. Our actions are judged and then we pay the price. In this myth, God or one of his attendants then takes us to heaven or hell, which is the reward or punishment for our actions.

The *Tibetan Book of the Dead* gives a common description of "the Judgment":

Listen. That thou art suffering so cometh from thine own karma; it is not due to anyone else's: it is by thine own karma.... Pray earnestly...that will protect thee.... The Good Genius [Higher Self] who was born...with thee will come now and count out thy good deeds with white pebbles, and the Evil Genius [one's lower, or shadow nature]...will come and count out thy evil deeds with black pebbles. Thereupon, thou wilt be greatly frightened, awed, and terrified and wilt tremble.... The Lord of Death will say, 'I will consult the mirror of karma.' So saying, he will look in the Mirror, wherein every good and evil act is vividly reflected.... Then [one of the attendants] of the Lord of Death will place *round thy neck* [the chakra of separation/judgment] a rope and drag thee along; he will cut off thy head, extract thy heart, pull out thy intestines...but thou wilt be incapable of dying. Although thy body be hacked to pieces, it will revive again...be not frightened; ...tell no lies; fear not the Lord of Death.

Thy body being a mental body is incapable of dying even though beheaded and quartered. In reality, thy body is of the nature of voidness [absolute, unmanifest being]; thou needest not be afraid. The Lords of Death are thine own *hallucinations*.... In reality, there are no such things.... Act so to recognize this.... Meditate upon the samadhi.... If thou does not know how to meditate, then merely analyze with care the real nature of that which is frightening thee. In reality, it is not formed into anything, but is a Voidness.... By merely recognizing [this]... thou art certain to obtain perfect Emancipation....[1]

The book *Psychedelic Experience* explains:

The judgment vision may come: the Third Bardo blame game.... A judgment scene is a central part of many religious systems, and the visions can assume various forms. Westerners are most likely to see it in the well-known Christian version. The Tibetans give a psychological interpretation to this as to all the other visions. The Judge, or Lord of Death, symbolizes conscience itself in its stern aspect of impartiality and love of righteousness. The "Mirror of Karma" (the Christian Judgment Book), consulted by the Judge, is memory. In all Tibetan systems of yoga, realization of the Voidness is the one great aim.[2]

As with most of the *Tibetan Book of the Dead*, the discourse can be looked at multidimensionally, as well as for the symbols within it, such as *judgment, hell, torture*, etc.

In the context of this book, separation and judgment are karmic themes of our emotional body used by the ego to show ourselves how we create illusion and thus separate ourselves from the highest reality.

"The Lords of Death" are the hallucinations of the emotional body, the "maya" we *think* is real. We have created the stage to play out our programming of what is good and bad. The judgment scene is a performance of what we *think* is our condition in life. Consequently, many of us are very harsh in our opinions of ourselves. Having lived in separation from God for what seems to be a very long time, we conjure up ample evidence as to why life has been so hard, so empty of blessing. Unfortunately, we often forget about the goodness we have created and all the good deeds we have performed. Somehow, in our harshness, an act of kindness never quite balances an act of selfishness. We tend to cling to the guilt, adamantly sentencing ourselves to even more suffering, so much so that we've come to depend upon it. We have great difficulty asking for forgiveness, mercy, and unconditional love—the very qualities we attribute to God—even though this spiritual energy will purge us of our illusion. Our inability to ask requires us to continue the journey of karma, even though it takes us into the torture of hell where eventually the lessons are learned, the purgation is complete, and we transcend our hallucination and come back into clear light.

It is interesting that in Tibetan philosophy the experience of hell is temporary, never permanent. Permanence is only a quality of the *highest* reality. Hell is not everlasting; it does have a function though: that of purging the ignorance of the ego. As we all know, pain and suffering are the result of those actions that identify us with separation from God. Previously, we saw the torture of judgment as the pangs of our own conscience. Enlightenment frees us from identification with the world of form so that we become permanently conscious of the formless. Pain and suffering are transcended and the bliss of the void is all that remains.

Along the same lines, the symbol of the Mirror of Karma is significant. It is the tool by which we come into consciousness and out of denial. Without the mirror we would be lost in our suffering without knowing the cause. The pain of the past would create confusion, allowing our ego to hold on to its sense of self, and remain strong in its defense of the status quo. The mirror of memory allows us now to proceed with either liberation or purgation, and regardless of which we choose, we continue the evolutionary process of growth of consciousness.

The mirror allows us to see clearly our acts of judgment (we don't need God to judge us) and the corresponding guilt that has crystallized our sense of ego and its need to play out suffering through the polarity of victim/victimizer.

If, in the mirror, we see acts that we judge to be "good" or godlike, then we are "sentenced" to move on to higher realms, coming closer to God. Yet we still have an ego and it is still identified with the reflection in the mirror of memory: "Oh, what a good father I was," or "I was the best composer in the land," or "I never harmed anyone." Even if "good" karma may have accumulated and no "bad" karma incurred, ignorance of Self still predominates, even though life may be perceived as being "blessed."

When we look in the mirror and see nothing, when there is no ego to see, no memory with which we are identified, the karmic slate is clean. We see the infinite reflection of the void, the formless. We no longer ride the wheel of life and death.

The Endless Cycle

Emotionally, the theme of separation/judgment creates an unfolding of powerful karma. Separation and judgment are always connected; one creates the other. Once the energy of separation is felt, judgment creates polarities: good/bad, right/ wrong. Judgment then leads to guilt. Regardless of how self-righteous we may feel, there is a consciousness of the effect of judgment.

If the situation is one of self-judgment where we have judged ourself as wrong, bad, stupid, etc., then close at hand we will be feeling guilt or remorse about our act of will. Guilt is an insidious energy that cripples us in one way or another; we take it on as a consequence of separation/judgment. The next step of this cycle is the infamous programming of we human beings and our institutions, which demands punishment when there is guilt. Punishment does not alleviate the suffering of our actions; it only produces more suffering by creating deeper and deeper imprints of victimization. The more we are punished, the more we are victimized. (It's interesting that in many cultures, the punishment of death was administered by closing down the throat chakra: by hanging, the guillotine, the blade, or even poison.)

If we look at the separation/judgment sequence, whether it be in a single lifetime or throughout many lifetimes, the karmic pattern is clear: separation/judgment eventually leads to self-created suffering, a manifestation of our self-perpetuated attempt to pay off debt. Hell then becomes the ultimate source of our need to maintain our separation through punishment. Aldous Huxley wrote, "... man's capacity to crave more violently than any animal for the intensification of his separateness results in moral evil [judgment] and the sufferings which moral evil inflicts.... Hell is total separation from God, and the devil is the will to that separation."[3]

We manifest hell in our lives by perpetuating the theme of separation/judgment. The throat chakra is where we hold this theme in our body. Being in the chakra of communication, this theme is the major blockage to our ability to communicate inwardly and outwardly and therefore prevents us from the experience of communion. Suffering engenders more suffering, adding layer upon layer to the negative themes that polarize life. This can only repeat until the vicious cycle is broken. The flow chart looks like this:

SEPARATION → JUDGMENT → GUILT → PUNISHMENT → VICTIM

One of the most powerful techniques for breaking this sequence is through the spiritual energy of *forgiveness*. This energy is divinely empowered with the ability to transform our "mistakes" into "teachings." Having grown, the event of the past is dissolved. *Forgiveness is the spiritual energy that releases us from the past and brings us into the clarity of the present moment.* It brings us out of guilt, judgment and separation. The result is arriving back home to the Self; here is love, the unifier of life. So the flow chart looks like this:

SEPARATION → JUDGMENT → GUILT → PUNISHMENT → VICTIM

↳ FORGIVENESS ←↙

↳ SELF-LOVE → SPIRIT

When we find ourself in a state of judgment and rising guilt, instead of following the program of punishment, we choose forgiveness. Of course, this must be a spiritual experience; forgiveness only on a superficial level is not potent enough. We must feel it from Spirit. Only then can it challenge our concept of God the Punisher. If we hold a fundamental belief that God is our judge then the way of punishment will persist. But if we are able to forgive another, to be compassionate and merciful to one who has hurt us, *then God must be at least as merciful as we*—for how can God be less merciful than we are?

On the level of Spirit, there is only unity—no polarity of judgment. God is perfection and God is everything; so all that is *within* space/time *is* perfect. Everything happens within the perfection of God—even that which we judge as bad or wrong. Our delusion is only temporary.

If we expand our consciousness to infinity, we can then release our distortion of reality. Judgment is no longer possible. Where there is no judgment, there is no separation; only the unity remains. Forgiveness brings us back to the unity of Self-love. It opens communication and brings us back to communion.

With forgiveness, the throat chakra opens powerfully, allowing the rush of spiritual energy into the third eye and upward through the crown, bringing us greater enlightenment. The throat chakra becomes the gateway linking our body (earth) and Higher Mind (heaven), the form and the formless. The communication of the lower chakras with the head chakras and the heavenly chakras results when we clear the themes of the throat and the gate opens to higher consciousness and the clarity of unity.

John's Session

The following session is an example of how our Higher Self uses the multidimensionality of our ego-concept to break through the illusions of self; this then allows our true spiritual nature to clear the throat chakra of the theme of separation/judgment. John journeys into realms of past karma, viewing the different dimensions of himself in the cycle of the victim/victimizer. His emotional body uses this vicious cycle to perpetuate his separation from God. To break the limited view of our ego and expand our perspective of who we truly are gives us the possibility of returning to the radiant light of self-love.

John: *I feel myself moving deep inside my throat chakra. The tightness I felt initially is diminishing. It's more expansive now—actually it feels very pleasant, more open, easier to talk.*

Facilitator: Use that openness to express everything that is happening, everything you feel. Go into it.

John: *It's mainly body sensations of good feelings. Everything is opening, expanding, becoming more fluid. The whole body is open and flowing...* (Pause)

Facilitator: What's happening?

John: *Images are coming into focus now. It was just streamers of colors slowly coming into human forms. I see an elderly woman, maybe seventy or eighty years old, holding a baby in her lap with her other arm around a woman in her late thirties or early forties. I see she's a grandmother with her daughter and her granddaughter. They're all smiling, happy, but there's something about the old woman, something very familiar. Let me see here....*
    Uh-huh, I get it! It's me, I'm the grandmother. I see it in the eyes. Those are my eyes, my consciousness. It feels so normal to be that woman, to be the mother of that daughter, to be a mother for most of my life—that mother energy—so feminine, so caring, so nurturing, watching my child grow, watching her have a little girl, as if we were clones of each other—not clones, but archetypes of "woman." I don't see any other children or men, just the three generations of women, independent of time or culture. It feels so real, as if it's happening now, yet my mind says this must be a past life or something.

Facilitator: It doesn't matter if it's a past life or not—just be with it. What happens?

John: *The women are there on the left, and now another image is forming on my right. It's a teenage boy about sixteen or seventeen with jet black hair and those same blue-grey eyes— my eyes again. It's me. He has shorts on and no shirt, just laying in soft green grass watching the clouds drift by. He* *looks like he's deep in thought, as if he's pondering the universe—wondering what the clouds are, why the sky is blue, where the wind comes from—totally intrigued by nature.*

Now I see a young woman, blonde, her hair braided, with a white cotton or linen dress on, quite beautiful, very natural. God, those same eyes—what's going on here? All these people are me!

Facilitator: Stay with it. Your Higher Self wants to show you these aspects of yourself.

John: *She is so attractive, naturally sensual. The top of her dress is unbuttoned to her full breasts. It must be a hot day. She's just walking along a mountain stream. She has a purple flower in her hair. She's singing to herself. She stops suddenly and listens, looks to her right where there's a sound—some notes of a flute maybe. She sees a fawn appear out of the bushes with white speckles on her coat. The deer just walks up to me as if we were good friends, then another baby deer and her mother come running out of the forest to us. I'm surrounded by these beautiful creatures. They even lick me like a bunch of dogs. I'm ecstatic, playing. It's so, so natural, like a dream. I feel their fur, the coarseness of their tongues, those big brown eyes. The funny thing is that the other figures are always there, kind of like a split screen in my mind. I'm with myself simultaneously—all my selves are coexisting together.*

Now another image. It must be a man, forty or fifty. Long beard, partly grey—and of course the same eyes. It looks like there's a scar or burned area on his neck. He has darker skin, maybe Indian or Tibetan, dressed in a maroon robe like in Tibet. He's picking herbs in a mountain field. He has a cloth bag, a knife, and a digging stick. He talks to the plants, and they talk to him. He must be an herbalist/healer.

The images just keep coming. I'm amazed. I see all these

people at once—these sessions are incredible. How does the mind do this? I've never experienced this before.

Facilitator: What image comes now?

John: *Well...this one doesn't seem to fit. It's not so nice...to say the least....*

Facilitator: Speak it out. What's happening?

John: *Well, I see myself laughing. I'm laughing at this naked woman who's tied down, tied to stakes in the ground. She's sobbing, terrified, and all I do is laugh. I have this sick, disturbed energy. I enjoy this game; I enjoy her suffering....*
   Then I slowly, deliberately rape her—she screams in my ear and I like it, it turns me on. I like to see her struggle. Then I lie down beside her; she's sobbing again. Every once in a while she asks me why I'm doing this to her, but the question never really pierces my heart. I lie there feeling a mixture of pleasure and pain.
   Then the scene retreats a bit, and I see that the woman I have raped is very similar to the image of me as the young woman with the deer and the grandmother when she was young and my daughter and the granddaughter when she was older and the boy. This is one time-line of the boy when he was older. (Tears)

Facilitator: What do you feel?

John: *It's so sad. It's a tragedy—the suffering we create...*

Facilitator: Go into it. What's this suffering?

John: *It's this addiction to the victim and the victimizer. I see* *myself victimizing myself. I see the masculine energy abusing the feminine, just like this planet has done to itself.* (Tears) *I'm not just one or the other, but I'm caught in it nevertheless. It's so tragic, so stupid! It's hard to talk. My throat is all congested with mucus.*

Facilitator: Bring your attention to your throat. Be with it.

John: *I bring light, a violet light there, like amethyst crystal light. It's clearing, now more open.*

My Higher Self comes into form as a shimmering crystal sword with a golden hilt. The sword is for cutting loose this ignorance, this illusion I live, we live. The sword, in the past, has been a weapon that caused suffering. Now it's an instrument for healing.

I see clearly all of the lifetimes. It's funny, but during the rape scene, the images of me faded out; it was the only time that happened. Now they're all back in view, even the victimizer man. The sword comes back to the center of the circle and all the people are gathered around, all aspects of me facing inward. I can see all of their faces.

The sword creates a radiance, a white light, and now I see myself as I am now. I walk into the middle, into the center of the circle. I take the sword in my hand, and I feel such a surge of energy through my body. (As he says this, John's body convulses. It seems to start at his feet and ripple up through his body to his head. His body jerks and he slightly bounces up and down on the table.)

It's powerful, but clear....

Facilitator: What's happening?

John: *I take the sword and I walk up to the grandmother first and hold the sword between us, illuminating us. She says, "I* *am you—just love your family. " Then I walk to the boy and he says, "I am you—in the innocence, life is such a wonder. "* (John's body jerks again on the table.)

Then I walk up to the young woman in white; she smiles and says, "I am you, Nature is you, and Nature loves you. " (Tears.)

I see the Tibetan man; he says, "I am you, you have seen me before. " Now I remember this man from a dream of three or four years ago. He says, "There will be suffering in this world, and that's one reason we are here—to heal, to be of service. "

Then I come to the victimizer and hold the sword up again. He just looks at me in silence. I look into his eyes; they change. Now they're more like my eyes. I know he represents the dark side in me, in this world, in the grand scheme of things. He maintains the polarities. He says, "I am you, let me teach you how to love yourself. " (John's body convulses again, and his breathing is very fast for about two to three minutes.)

I move to the center again. I feel my spiritual energy swirling around me. The sword is still radiating. And then the circle closes in. All my different aspects move closer until I'm spinning really fast. It's incredible. They spin into me; I spin into myself. But it's not as I see myself now, in this body, as John, but I'm more expansive, less defined. Now I'm just light. It feels so amazing. I feel what it's like to be light—just light.... (Silence)

(End of session)

Beyond Duality

Universal Mind exists in oneness, *beyond* duality, *beyond* the field of opposites. When Universal Mind manifests into our world with all its individual minds and separate lives, then the dualistic field of opposites becomes relevant. Here is where our experience is judged as good or bad, to be of the light or of the shadow. These opposites coexist as two sides of the same coin.

As Larry Dossey states in his book, *Recovering the Soul*:

... the light and shadow exist together as rightful parts of a whole. If we hold to the light and deny the shadow, we will not understand the whole when we experience it, and we will be assailed with the overwhelming force of tragedy, disease, and death. Only through the conscious recognition of the complexity of the whole can we escape being devastated when bad things happen.[4]

Dossey's statement is important. When "bad" things happen, the emotional body and its voice, the ego, experience the event in terms of the localized, narcissistic self. We identify with it personally. This action creates more separation, and where there is separation, there will always be judgment creating the polarity of good and bad.

Because "bad things" cause suffering, they have a tendency to create more constriction, or a collapse into *local-mind* rather than allowing consciousness to expand into unboundedness. If we can maintain our awareness of nonlocal mind, the collapse will be eased and our recovery back into nonattachment will be faster. We will learn our lesson more clearly; the situation will expand us out of our localized, personal viewpoint so that we can see the event as part of the perfection of the cosmic plan.

In his book, Dossey uses an example of one of India's great mystics and gurus, Sri Ramana Maharshi, who died of cancer in 1950:

... the pain was so great that his moans frequently prevented his devotees from sleeping... the pain in his body was obvious to anyone. And at night he seemed to lose control over himself.... His devotees... asked him to explain what seemed to be a great contradiction: How could a God-realized man such as he, freed eternally from the rounds of birth and death, still feel pain, suffer, and cry out for relief? Did not the enlightened state preclude such misery?

When he heard this question, Maharshi broke into a large smile. With love and compassion he replied, "You take this body for Bhagavan (God) and attribute suffering to him. What a pity! I am the Self. If the hand of the Jnani were cut with a knife, there would be pain, as with anyone else, but because he is not identified with the body, he remains in bliss despite the pain."[5]

Even the enlightened person feels pain yet they are beyond attachment: *in* the world but not *of* the world. Pain, suffering, and what we might call "bad luck" do happen to all of us. The test is whether we identify with the action or situation (karma) or whether we maintain the freedom of unboundedness in the midst of it. The liberated self experiences life as the witness—feeling, observing, and thinking without being overshadowed or lost in the experience.

In relation to the dynamics of communication, the ideal is to be in the world, communicating to the world of form through our mind, body, and emotion, yet simultaneously communing with Spirit, being one with God, embodying that freedom within the boundaries of form and daily life. *Communication* connects us to the flow of time and space. *Communion* anchors us into the infinite. Regardless of what happens in the material world, we are eternal in the arms of

God.

What is the purpose of life?
To come to realize God in everything,
to perceive the Divine in all life,
in every moment of being.
By knowing the Divine,
we live life in love.
Being unattached,
flowing with the moment,
one with love.
And by being love, we give it,
we teach it, and experience it in communion.[6]

Trust and Surrender

Our judgment arises out of the illusory ground state of separation. It is lonely living in the "reality" of separation. We view ourselves as being on our own, separate, different from everything else. Naturally there arises a deep survival instinct. Our genetic need to survive is as ancient as our ego's need to be in separation. *Survival engenders judgment, and it is cautious of any threat.* If we look at the list of people, groups, and beliefs that we judge, we will see the common thread of our judgment. To survive, we feel we need to control our world. If anything challenges that control it is viewed as a threat. Judgment targets that which we think could threaten our sense of the way life should be. Secure in our self-righteousness, we will defend that singular viewpoint, often unto suffering, sometimes unto death.

Our judgments always polarize us. The republican judges the democrat, the fascist judges the communist, the rich judge the poor, the strong judge the weak, the good judge the bad, the young judge the old, one polarity judges the opposite, and on and on and on... As long as yin judges yang or vice-versa, the differences cause separation which causes conflict. When our differences are grounded in unity, our system is enriched and benefited and there is no conflict.

We cannot deny the reality that we are each living in a body and that our bodies hold the memory of survival, i.e., our needs for food, water, shelter, and other requirements of life. If someone threatens our survival, then limits encroach upon our unlimitedness. But if we are unbounded, nothing can encroach. To be unbounded requires *trust, surrender,* the *Big Leap.*

Trust means to let go of our scenarios of limitation and the thoughtforms of "not enough." Trust returns us to our innate knowing of abundance and our willingness to let go. Trust says yes to following our bliss and to the knowing that everything flows in cosmic perfection.

Surrender is letting go of control and the willful need to change our "imperfect" world. Being one with God is surrendering to God's will—"...*thy* will be done,"—and not being attached to the outcome. Surrender is being at peace and in the moment. Pleasure and pain may come but we go on, forever, witnesses to what is. If God *is* everything, then God is also present in the perfection of our pain. If we are willing to surrender to pain, then we are ready for the *Big Leap.* Surrender is coming into the realization that "what is" *is* perfect. We *are* at one with perfection.

In the breaking of patterns, changing the rules, doing the unexpected, the world is relative; there is no right or wrong unless we judge it so. *The only reality is God consciousness; from that anything is possible.*

Given this, how do we live? What do we do? We attempt to live in love and surrender to the moment. When we choose to act, we act in service to God, in honor of God, and to promote God-consciousness in our thoughts and through our words and deeds. To do this is not to get lost in the action but to get found by God!

Good and bad are only relevant when we have stepped into the game of life. By stepping in, we experience the objects of perception from our particular point of view. The freedom comes when we maintain Self and witness the game—we experience the game but are not part of it.

Life allows us to experience the swing from exquisite bliss to exquisite pain. We maintain Self while we watch the game unfold. We have come into body to learn freedom, to learn to experience feelings without losing ourself to them.

> *I feel pain to know I'm beyond pain.*
> *I feel loss to know I'm beyond loss.*
> *I feel emotion to know I'm beyond emotion.*
> *I feel experience to know I'm beyond experience.*
> *I am Pure Consciousness, flat, unbounded, eternal...*
> *Let me use time to be my Self in the flow of life.*[7]

Near Death Experiences as Example

One of the most fascinating and transforming experiences for human beings is the near-death experience (NDE). Recently there has been an increase in documentation and research on this topic. Dr. Kenneth Ring's impressive book, *The Omega Project*, clearly describes these experiences and their effects on people's lives.

What I find most interesting are the similar descriptions of spiritual virtues these people experience during their NDEs. The case studies are rich in encounters with beings of light who radiate unconditional love, acceptance, and compassion.

But most importantly, NDEs are excellent examples of non-judgment and communion. One of Dr. Ring's subjects describes her experience thusly:

> ... and "God" was within the brightness. I felt loved beyond all judgment, an "agape" type of love, and completely accepted. This "God" communicated to me—no words, just kind of pushed knowledge into me—that I had a rough past but he/she was delighted at my handling of my life, and that I was OK...[8]

Another person says,

> ...I saw what I believed to be a face...I cannot remember tears, but if they were possible, the emotion was so strong that they would have been falling like a waterfall. I looked upon the face again and I was filled with a feeling of love, peace, and knowledge... I think if I took one thing away from this experience, it was that the most powerful force that we all have is love, and before this I had no idea what love was, only what I had been shown in the world.[9]

As Dr. Ring writes,

> The theme of love—self-love (in the sense of self-acceptance), love for others, love for the planet, love for the divine cosmos—is in fact the constant refrain in these NDE hymns. NDEers, almost without exception, are wont to say that it was the message of love that was the most important gift and indeed the very essence of the encounter. And it is this same love that they wish to make known and share with others, truly to give the most precious thing that they themselves

have received.[10]

It becomes obvious that God is love and love is God. The state of nonjudgment these experiences exemplify contrasts dramatically with our incarnational predicament of self-judgment. This self-created and seemingly eternal problem of separation/judgment is part of the karmic package we accept when we come into the human body. This separation/judgment theme becomes identified with life to such an extent that we have to flirt with death to see another perspective. It is as if our divine nature had been tainted, resulting in the shame of a "fallen angel." Fortunately, the call of the Divine attracts us home; our judgment is our only impediment to liberation. Once we release this illusion, our life dawns with new vigor and new purpose and we become conscious of Divine Love.

7

∞

Communication into Communion

Communion in Bali

In April 1991, my wife, Rachel, and I participated in a spiritual healing conference on the island of Bali, Indonesia. We were there to talk about the symbol of the Divine Child and its use in psychospiritual healing. The conference was powerful but the place was even more powerful, truly a sacred site. The energies were anything but subtle—what was it that made this place different? I had heard various theories, all of which made some sense, but it wasn't until early one morning that I discovered a different viewpoint that touched me deeply.

The sun was rising and I sat in a beautiful Balinese temple watching the priest perform a *puja* (ritual ceremony). His soft melodic chanting was perfectly integrated with his every movement and gesture. He sprinkled water and I felt a wave of coolness to the approaching daytime heat. We offered a flower to the gods and I felt thanksgiving, then a pinch of rice and I felt a nourishing satiation at my core. The chanting reminded me of tradition, of all the teachers who had come before. My heart was full of appreciation.

The priest waved sticks of incense, and I felt the currents of sweetness purify my consciousness. Then he lit a small ball of white powder and the smell of camphor transmuted out a bright light and my inner awareness became brighter and clearer.

It was a crystal clarity, as if my mind had become a pure quartz crystal. Looking through it brought me the realization of what an enlightened consciousness must be like. All the static of my mind ceased. The smoke cleared, my focus sharpened, and the screen of my mind became alive and fully awakened. Stillness became the background of my senses; the stillness held within me a sense of deep pleasure.

With his sparkling eyes, the Balinese priest seemed to see beyond the superficial, down into the dish of holy water. Each time he bowed his head, unknowingly his beard would dip into the cup of water—a new way to sprinkle his offerings. I smiled inside, watching the adorable performance.

As the ceremony continued, time was of no concern. The priest's influence was easily transmitted to me and I became aware that the energies were communicated to all the celestial realms as well. There was a giving and receiving of energy, and this *puja* was a wonderful way to give thanks, appreciation, and honor to those beyond the veil. Each gesture was symbolic and each symbol was alive with energy, thereby opening pathways of connection.

The symbolic expanded my consciousness. The temple, the environment, the very land came alive with the bridging of energy across the dimensions. Then I got it; then I knew why Bali was so special: it was the generations of worship, the activation of the air, water, and earth of this place through the symbolic and mythic technologies of communication. Spirit was *infused* into the forms here. It reminded me of how other cultures have become conscious of the unseen worlds. In Bali, there is an openness to both the worlds of light and darkness. The demons as well as the devas are given attention. The communication is not judgmental. The dark side is perceived as necessary, or the ignored spirit gets angry or malicious in reaction. I felt this was an important teaching: that if we ignore the undesirable, or lock it into denial, then that withholding of consciousness may have negative consequences.

The *puja*, like any traditional ceremony, is symbolic and structured to *open communion from the subtle to the gross levels of awareness*. The offering of an ablution, a flower, some rice, or a stick of incense is about exchanging energy to nourish, purify, or set the intention of consciousness, as if to say, "I'm here, I honor your life, needs, and perspective." It is acknowledging our existence with compassionate awareness—hopefully as an offering rather than for the asking for a boon or as a way to avoid suffering. *Proper intention is an important key to ritual*. *Yagya* is a sacramental action that benefits or supports personal and/or universal evolution. On the highest level, yagya offers loving kindness for the sheer joy of the giving.

After the *puja* was over, I felt the gods had given me a great personal gift, a teaching about yet another form of communication.

First Open the Heart!

The experience of communion is dependent upon an open heart chakra, where the vital energy can flow up from the lower chakras, through the heart, and rise into the throat chakra for expression. Since the chakras are the energetic bridges between the subtle bodies and the physical body, they can channel high-vibratory spiritual energies into manifestation. The heart chakra plays a key role in channeling Spirit into matter, spiritual love into relationship. To understand this function, it is important to understand the energetics of the heart chakra.

In Chinese medicine the heart holds the *shen*, which is one of those indescribable concepts that means something like

"Spirit." It is that energy that enlivens us, the consciousness that radiates from deep within. Sometimes we can see it clearly emanating in someone's eyes when they are awake and aware.

The heart chakra controls the area of the chest which includes the heart and lung organs. If the function of these organs or their corresponding meridians is unbalanced or blocked, then a host of emotional issues come into play. An imbalanced heart results in anxiety, restlessness, and disassociation, revealing an unsettled or disturbed spirit. A blockage to Spirit is a blockage to the flow of the spiritual within our life, which further separates us from unity. A healthy heart is filled with love, compassion, joy, and laughter.

The lungs and lung meridian are the master controllers of the body's energy. When blocked, the energy declines, weakens, and moves us into a depressive state of emptiness. The karmic themes of the lungs are of sadness, grief, aloneness, isolation, helplessness, hopelessness, powerlessness, defeat—all the ingredients of the "depression complex."

Since the heart chakra is the chakra of relationship, *it must give energy.* Just as the heart pumps blood throughout the body, giving energy and nourishment to our living system, it is also vital to nourish our outer world, where relationship is the key function. The heart must give energy to relationships which bring us into life as part of life. If it does not, we are not being nourished and we die—just as if the lungs were to stop functioning, or the heart to stop beating, we would die.

We are all seeking love because love is our lifeblood; without it our vital energy ebbs away—our presence becomes superficial and ineffectual and more committed to the status quo of unconsciousness.

Love is the supreme spiritual energy. When our heart loves another, there is an immediate attraction that pulls us closer, into greater intimacy. Love always unifies because *love is God and God is love.* Being in love is being in God. The heart is vitally important; *it is the doorway to the Divine.* Opening the heart is opening to God's love and ultimately to the experience of communion.

On the other hand, if the heart is blocked, love and Spirit are overshadowed and we find ourselves in the aloneness of separation and the suffering of the closed heart.

The important question is, why does the heart close down? The essence of the answer always centers on the fear of pain. Instinctively, we try to withdraw from heartbreak or to avoid, defend against, or escape painful situations. After experiencing the imprint of pain, we may keep our heart closed as a way to defend against our unknown future. We condition ourselves to maintain our armor, to respond to pain by repeatedly running away or numbing it out—in other words, by going unconscious.

In shutting down our emotional body, we not only lock in the imprints of our past pain, but our karmic theme acts like a magnet that continues to resonate the energy out into our world, attracting the very situations that perpetuate our karma. We may think that the shutdown is helping but in reality it is an act of avoidance, the ego's way of perpetuating the status quo that keeps us from resolution and releasing the "magnet."

There is an effective way of dealing with our suffering. Buddhist psychology gives us the technique of *turning into the pain*, which of course is just the opposite of our instinctual response. By allowing consciousness to gently move toward the *source* of the pain, we provide an opportunity to perceive the purpose of the pain and learn the lesson at hand. As consciousness penetrates the energetic attachment of the issue, there is an immediate movement of energy resulting in resolution and cessation of pain. To experience the healing influence of greater consciousness requires us to look at old pains that reside within us. As we learn to deal consciously with our suffering, instead of letting it control us, we become the masters of our destiny. This empowerment inspires us to move forward without fear, firm in our knowing that we can handle anything that may come.

The Experience of Communion

The experience of true communion is one of unified connection. The power of love energetically brings us out of separation and into oneness with another and ultimately with Spirit. Communion is the state of being in love in which attachment has no meaning and dependency no relevance. Communion is beyond the world of duality and only exists in the Divine Heart. Being in love does not require an object, for it is a state of being, transcendentally unbounded. The heart is the gateway and love is the unifying energy that pulls us through the open gate into the infinity of Self. Opening our heart is a sacred step in our evolution, the last challenge to illusion. Once our heart opens its divine love, no judgment can remain for long, and Spirit consciously takes us into an eternal embrace, our communion complete.

Our moments of communion with a lover are the moments when our individuality falls away and our profound intimacy has no boundaries. Two are now one; any separation has been lost in the merging. The bodies are so close that we no longer know where we begin or end. Within our consciousness, individual thought ceases and a telepathic connection allows the two to think as one, feel as one, be one.

Communion is not limited to the experience between lovers or mother and child or dear friends, but can also be experienced between ourself and anything outside or inside our field of perception. There are moments—say while working in the garden—when our consciousness reaches out and powerfully connects with a daisy and all of a sudden, time stands still, our sense of localized self (ego) disappears, and we perceive ourself as the daisy—not only connected, but now one with the flower, enthralled in its perfection. Spirit, which is omnipresent, is now being perceived as the flower, which is ourself. The divinity of the daisy has bridged the gap of separation and drawn us into communion with the Self— which is the daisy or the rose or the broccoli plant.

Communion is the experience of losing our sense of who we think we are—the constructs of our ego's personality— and revealing the soul essence that is common to all creation. When *our* Spirit essence is experienced, we open to the Spirit essence in the other and we are able to let go of the illusory distance so that we can merge. Duality creates a gap between the subject and the object of perception. But when communion is experienced, the gap disappears.

The ultimate form of communion occurs in the state of enlightenment as we merge with Spirit and experience Spirit as our True Self. Our ego expands to include a new concept of self. We are consciously married to Spirit on the level of the Absolute. Communion is both an experience of the Absolute in the silence of meditation and a unity consciousness, coexisting with waking, dreaming, or sleeping states. We perceive Spirit as *ourself* which is never lost to our consciousness. All perception mirrors Spirit because all that we experience is part of what we are. Therefore, communion with Spirit is eternal; separation is no longer valid in this state of knowledge.

Communion brings recognition of the highest reality, the unity of Spirit. The state of communion is that experience of oneness that is our source, our sustenance, and our eternal resting place. We are created from it, maintained by it in our life, in our body. Through the experience of that unified state, we can dissolve all illusion and barrier to its actuality as it attracts us home again.

At any moment, the possibility exists for us to experience, to know, and to make permanent our communion with Spirit— to *enlighten* our sense of self with that which is truly real.

Communion and The Tibetan Book of the Dead

One of the great moments in our cycle of life is the moment of death, the releasing of our physical body as we transcend the Earth plane and experience the subtler dimensions of Spirit. One of the sacred guides for this transition from body to spirit to rebirth is the *Bardo Thodol*, the *Tibetan Book of the Dead*. It is used as a set of instructions to help us experience communion with the "clear light" of Spirit—in Buddhist terminology, the *Dharma-Kaya*, or the Divine Body of Truth, that primordial state of uncreatedness, of the supramundane All-consciousness—Buddhahood.

As the moment of death arrives, the individual soul experiences its absolute nature—unbounded, infinite bliss, *Brahman*. This is an opportunity for us, at our first stage of initiation, to realize that we can experience our essence as the unity consciousness of Spirit.

By recognizing our True Self, we become united and liberation is achieved.

Supposedly, at death we have the possibility of shedding all forms—our body, memories, emotions, viewpoints—and we merge into communion with Spirit, but usually the forms hold us prisoner. These "thoughtforms" are created by our karma to show us what is not yet resolved within our finite consciousness.

The second stage of the initiation of Spirit is to become conscious of our emotional issues and release them into the Light. This period is known as the *Chonyid Bardo*, a stage of manifest karmic attachments with the imagery, feelings, and play of karmic illusion, which we still perceive as being real. The illusions can seem incredibly intense, equivalent to a manifest psychosis; yet in Spirit, there is no death. We are afforded the opportunity to let go of these hallucinations and move back into communion. This stage demands that we communicate with that which was previously repressed and unresolved.

If the second stage is unsuccessful, we proceed to the third stage, the *Sidpa Bardo*, which takes us into rebirth and a continuation of our karmic cycle. Even in the Sidpa Bardo—or for that matter, at any point in the cycle, whether incarnate or not—we can attain liberation. Consciousness is required. We must awaken to illusion and communicate, which in this context means to activate our consciousness in order to release the grip of the illusion of time, space, and its manifest forms thus allowing our consciousness to expand into Spirit.

The instructions state:

Whichever light shineth upon thee now, meditate upon it as being the Compassionate One; ...this is an exceedingly profound Art; it will prevent birth. Or whatsoever thy tutelary deity may be, meditate upon the form for much time, as being apparent yet nonexistent in reality, like a form produced by a magician. That is called the pure illusory form. Then let the [visualization of the] tutelary deity melt away from the extremities till nothing at all remaineth visible of it; and put thyself in the state of the Clearness and the Voidness—which thou canst not conceive as something—and abide in that state for a little while. Again meditate on the tutelary deity; again meditate upon the Clear Light: do this alternately. Afterwards, allow thine own intellect also to melt away gradually, beginning from the extremities.... In that state, birth will be obstructed and Perfect Enlightenment gained.[1]

The resolution of karma is the "work of life"; each lesson learned, each illusion dispelled, each fear overcome allows the opening of our consciousness to what is true. The opening to love is the opening to the spiritual. As we have seen, this is a process that continues whether we are embodied or not.

Any spiritual experience, whether it be through yoga, meditation, psychospiritual work, or even in psychedelic sessions, can help us transcend the patterns of the ego by releasing us from the subject-object duality of the world and into the unity of communion. Throughout time, there have been theoretical "maps" and instructions created for this inner journey. *The Tibetan Book Of the Dead* is perhaps more important to the *living* than to the dead in its purpose to free our attention from each successive stage of delusion and entanglement and guide us to the ever-present possibility of liberation. In the words of Timothy Leary, Ralph Metzner, and Richard Alpert (Ram Dass):

> The *Tibetan Book of the Dead* is ostensibly a book describing the experiences to be expected at the moment of death...during an intermediate phase...and during rebirth.... This however is merely the exoteric framework which the Tibetan Buddhists used to cloak their mystical teachings.... The esoteric meaning...*is that it is death and rebirth of the ego that is described,* not *that of the body*. Lama Govinda indicates this clearly in his introduction when he writes: "It is a book for the living as well as for the dying." The book's esoteric meaning is often concealed beneath many layers of symbolism. It was not intended for general reading. It was designed to be understood only by one

who was to be initiated personally by a guru into the Buddhist mystical doctrines, into the *pre-mortem* death/rebirth experience.[2]

The Awakened Heart

One of the steps toward communion is through a form of empathy, in which we experience a strong connection with another. In that moment, we know it's impossible to cause that person harm, either directly or indirectly. The reason for this is that we sense Spirit within them, which is nothing more than a reflection of Spirit within ourselves. Connection with Spirit *is* the essence of communion, although the emotional body may still be experienced as only *coexisting* with Spirit. Because our heart must be open in order to approach communion, we may feel vulnerable; or we may be open empathically—able to feel another's pain. Our open heart feels everything and it is expansive in its feeling. Our vulnerability is only temporary; it transforms into courage, which eventually creates invincibility. Although we continue to feel more and more, our attachments become less and less.

The *bodhicitta* in Buddhist tradition means the "awakened heart." It is the heart that courageously exposes itself and reveals itself to consciousness. The *bodhicitta* invites communion because, being so expansive, it takes the manifest universe into its infinity. Whether it experiences pleasure or pain, goodness or evil, the awakened heart is pure compassion. There is no judgment that can block its power. In oneness there is no selectivity; all life is welcome because in communion I am not separate.

On the road to attain *bodhicitta*, we experience all of our emotional body issues that have created a closed, fearful heart.

Our pain, being so strong, causes a natural defensiveness that attempts to protect or block us from anymore pain. We must pass through these experiences for they teach us wisdom.

As the heart awakens, we have a mixture of experiences. Our open heart may experience the high-vibrations of love, joy, compassion, even the merging into unity. But close at hand, we may also experience the old energies of pain, sorrow, and other variations on the themes of the constricted heart. Our opening can flood us with the purging of our old pain—a movement out of old memory. The pain must leave so the heart can heal. This is *not* new pain coming in; there is no need to trigger our old patterns of defensiveness. *Closing down the heart holds the pain inside. Opening the heart transforms it. If we could learn this one lesson, life would no longer hold us prisoner.*

As it heals, our open heart brings us moments of ecstasy and moments of sorrow, tremendous love and tremendous disappointment, the positive and the negative. Until we experience communion, duality is real—*preference* is the rule. In communion, only oneness is real—there are no preferences, for what *is* is perfect.

The Sanyama of Communion:
A Technique

Yogi Patanjali, the famous Indian teacher who lived sometime between 200 and 500 B.C., wrote what are called the Yoga Sutras. These are succinct formulas of consciousness that can stabilize and integrate our unbounded awareness into daily life. Each formula, or *sutra*, acts as a demonstration of how the formless can manifest into form while strengthening the benefit of the formless in our everyday life. In other words, the basis of these meditation practices is the integration and stabilization of the absolute divine awareness within each of us. Some know them as *siddhis* (divine perfections or powers), seemingly supernatural abilities such as levitation, psychic abilities, supernormal strength, etc. What is relevant to this discussion is the basis of the technique from which these phenomena arise. There are four parts to the technique.

1. *Dharana*—proper attention: this step is *the fixing of our attention on an object of perception.* Attention directs the consciousness toward something, whether it be a person we are talking to or some thought or form within us. If attention dissolves or wanders, the possibility of successful communication is blocked. For example, if we are attentive as we read a book then we are involved with the message and meaning is gained. But if our attention wanders then no meaning is gained and we must "wake up" before we can start the process again.

2. *Dhyana*—proper meditation: Dhyana is a bit more difficult to explain because words such as *meditation, concentration,* and *holding the attention* are inadequate to explain this step. *Dhyana is the application of consciousness in a steady but penetrating way.* It takes the attention *into* the object of perception, moving deeper and deeper into its essence. It allows the consciousness within the object to connect and merge with our consciousness.

I remember taking a classical music exam in college for which I was supposed to listen to a symphony and analyze its composition. Having never heard this piece before, it was totally confusing to me. I was unable to perceive the theme and

I felt lost in a cloud of confusion. My attention was quite lively as I listened but my mind wanted to give up in defeat. Even so, I held my attention, listening, deeper and deeper, going beyond the need to "figure it out." As soon as I had disengaged my intellect, I penetrated to the core of the music and the structure suddenly dawned on me in its entirety. It was both startling and awe-inspiring. I felt an expansion within me—a rapture. My mind then jumped in and said, "This is so obvious now. Why couldn't I have known this immediately?" My attention on the problem was not enough; I had to take it deeper, *beyond thinking*, which brings us to the third and most important step.

> 3. *Samadhi*—inner knowing: the subject of *samadhi* is a complex one, although I will try to simplify. In my example of the music exam, the moment I transcended the intellect I sank into a moment of *samadhi*, and as a result, my desire to know was fulfilled. *Dhyana* took my attention inward, holding it steady and vital, but transcendence was necessary. *Samadhi is that state of consciousness beyond thought.* It is an inner wakefulness—a state where I am conscious of pure consciousness: aware of pure awareness.

Simply thinking is too superficial. Going to the source of thought *with* our desire or *with* the object of perception allows the "other" to transcend to *its* source. That source being pure consciousness *is* our *common* source. Consciousness joining with consciousness creates a communion of subject and object, bringing realization to both. This realization has an internal effect on the perceiver—in my case, a feeling of expansiveness and rapture.

4. *Sanyama*: The first three steps culminate into the

forth step called *Sanyama*. *Sanyama is the "aha!" experience*. It takes us beyond the ego and into pure spiritual awareness. When the Higher Self consciousness comes into the problem, a desire, or an object of perception, its influence produces the dawning of realization and the cognition of understanding.

This "aha!" feeling has been studied by many neurophysiologists. They have shown there is a synchronization of brain-wave activity, indicating a harmonious and efficient functioning of the nervous system. This coherence of mind makes sense in terms of confusion being released and replaced by clarity and understanding.

In summary, first we bring our attention to the object. Then we take our attention deeper into it, not pushing or rushing, but gently *holding* our attention on the object, into transcendence with it, letting go, to its source. Having transcended thought and desire, we experience the pure consciousness of *samadhi*. As we come out, *sanyama* produces realization and fulfillment.

With regards to communication and communion, *sanyama* can be used as a model that can help develop our ability to succeed in our relationship to others and Self.

Communication requires *dharana* (attention) so that the flow of energy is perceived, and the two can connect and interact. *Dhyana* takes the attention deeper into the essence of another's feelings, into their message, so that we can understand more than just their words and actions. *Dhyana* takes us into communion with the other. *Samadhi* is the linking consciousness; it is the "ground state" of our interconnectedness. It is the unifying force that tears away all boundaries of separation. The two now experience the one.

Communion that is practiced, just like the practice of *sanyama*, develops and grows. It expands the state of consciousness further and further. As with all things, the experience of communion may be ecstatic, but then it is over and even our memory of it may fade. However, as we practice the "sanyama of communion," each experience integrates and stabilizes its everlasting quality which is none other than pure consciousness, the absolute state of existence. To use my favorite analogy, it is like putting a white cloth in yellow dye and then hanging the cloth in the sun to dry. As it dries, the yellow fades in the sun. So we put it back in the yellow dye, and then back into the sun to dry. This time, more of the yellow remains as less fades. We keep repeating this "formula" until the yellow color never fades and is permanent.

In the same way, the more we commune, the longer it lasts, until one day, communion becomes a permanent state of being. This is the same as *unity consciousness*, that state where the object of perception is perceived as the same as ourself. Whether it be a lover, a rose, a cloud, or a demon— all is one. Communion is self-perpetuating; it is the state of manifest unity consciousness.

Underwater Communion

In May of 1991, my wife, Rachel, and I spent a few weeks in Fiji doing some serious scuba diving from the dive boat *Pacific Nomad*. We didn't realize that we would be part of a group of divers who each had done no less than two hundred dives, compared to our ten. Nonetheless, we followed them into some of the best diving in the world, an experience that is practically indescribable.

One night, I went out with a small group of divers to explore a sheer wall that dropped to about four hundred feet. In the moonless night, the blackness was profound. We descended to a depth of about sixty feet and let the gentle current carry us along the wall. As always on a night dive, the underwater flora and fauna change dramatically as the nocturnal creatures came out to feed. The coral polyps swaying with the current, the colors and textures, all seem to be of another world. The coral kingdom is exquisitely beautiful in the aquamarine clarity of the daytime; at nighttime, it is even more spectacular. There are bizarre invertebrates, moray eels, and other coral life. I became absolutely mesmerized by this underwater world.

After half an hour of enchantment, I swam forty feet straight out from the wall—the deep water below me—and turned off my flashlight. I was stunned by the pitch black of this world. Here I was at least ten miles from the nearest island, several miles from the ship, with only a dinghy floating somewhere above. This feeling of being absolutely alone, floating there in the middle of the ocean sixty feet below the surface, simulates being in deep intergalactic space. There was only me and myself in the black silent isolation where only my breath distinguished life from death.

As I floated there, I realized that I could easily panic. What would happen if my light would not come on? Was I sinking beyond the safe limits of recovery? Was I drifting out of reach of the others? What would happen if my air shut off? Would there be anybody around to save me? I was taking a stupid risk that no diver should ever take. But instead of panic, I felt a calmness. The stillness of the water became my body and the darkness of the night turned my senses inward. All I could perceive was the omnipresence of that absolute stillness, the unboundedness of Self, that which is just pure being—no form, no movement, nowhere to go, nothing to do—just the eternal moment. Floating there motionless, hearing nothing, seeing nothing, and at moments not even breathing any more, my consciousness no longer had a container. Everything fell away; time no longer existed, and space was distorted into nothingness—no up or down, no sense of direction. I was left with nothing, yet I seemed to expand into everything.

I have no idea how long I floated there in the infinite ocean; suddenly though, my body jerked in an involuntary spasm, and I saw thousands of minute flashes of pale green light. I was surrounded in a shower of iridescence. My emotions felt like a surge of stardust, a flash of the initial catalyst of creation, an explosion that sets worlds into motion. "Let there be light" the darkness a perfect backdrop for this dance of light, then sparkling back into the silence of the blackness.

I waved my arms, and the phosphorescence came to life again, bathing me in its galactic splendor yet reminding me of the submarine universe. I played and played, now energized, fully alive as a spirit of light, creating waves of tiny stars, bringing light into being. After a few minutes, I stopped and came back to the silence, feeling restful after my joyous job of creation—as if I could understand God's need for a day of rest.

Yet my day only lasted a minute before I noticed in the unfathomable distance a different light. There were flashes, still green, but now the flashes were more pronounced, and they moved in a dance, up and down, zigzagging, in synchrony. There were five sets of flashing lights dancing in front of me. This wasn't the phosphorescence of microorganisms activated by my movements; this was something unexplainable.

My curiosity was intensely aroused. My mind searched in vain for an explanation. My heart rejoiced in the unexpected. My body wanted to dance with such grace and rhythm. Finally my mind won, and I turned on my flashlight. I saw that the lights were fish, flashlight fish, to be exact. They had come to bring me back into my body, back into the world as a human, reminding me that for now, I was just a visitor and it was time to be getting back to my fellow divers and the surface where

I belonged. Yet they communicated a deep insight to me, and as I surfaced, I realized that I had never really felt alone in my isolation; I was literally surrounded in the waters of being, and the experience opened me to true peace. The feeling penetrated my whole being and prepared me for what was yet to come. That experience revealed to me the field in which all energy communicates, beyond time and space.

8

Creating New Realities

Oneness in the Wind

The day had been busy; I had done almost nine hours of Deva sessions with clients. As I walked back to my house, the hammock seemed to be inviting me to rest under the cool shade of the trees. Lying down with the gentle swinging helped to clear my mind. I watched the rhythmic motion of the trees swaying in the wind.

As I sank deeper into myself, I noticed my consciousness expanding; this allowed me to observe with greater clarity and precision. Gradually even the air became visible; I watched it communicate with the trees; the wind shared its energy with the leaves that rustled in response. The Tibetan prayer flags hanging above me were activated by the wind and empowered to send their prayers of compassion to the far corners of the universe. The wind chimes and bells translated the energy of communication into a symphony that reverberated into infinity. The energy was everywhere, yet the wind itself could not be seen. It needed to connect with another to share its message.

In its wisdom, the wind does not guard its message; its own expansiveness carries its energy into all dimensions—a rippling wave of consciousness. It keeps all enlivened and empowered, then returns to stillness while maintaining its omnipresence.

As I lay there watching this cosmic lesson of nature, the

wind began to surround me in a refreshing embrace. My lungs filled with its gift of energy, sending vitality into my fatigued body. I remembered that in Chinese medicine the lungs are the master controller of energy of the body. To breathe is to be alive and vibrant. At this moment, the *ch'i* (vital energy) of the wind was the fundamental energy source for earth's life forms. By watching the wind's empowerment, I watched Spirit communicate with all things.

Relative and Absolute Reality

Creation is multidimensional; we have the ability to view life at different levels, from the superficial to the subtle. The multidimensional range of form exists within the relative field of creation. Each level has characteristics that can be described, from the round, red apple to the organic molecules that give it form. Each level has an integrity that gives us a different reality, a different expression. When we transcend the dimensions of form, we arrive at the formless, that transcendental level of pure potential—that unbounded, infinite field of Universal Mind that has within it the potential to create any form. Universal Mind, God, the Creator, is absolute, unchanging, omnipresent, and eternal. Thus the multidimensional creation has two aspects: 1) the relative field of *expressed* energy and matter—that which can be located in time and space; and 2) the *unexpressed* absolute, which is nonlocal and beyond time and space. The *relative* springs forth from the *Absolute*, yet the Absolute is home and source of all, silently unmanifest. The only rule of the Absolute is unity; the Absolute coexists in any manifestation of the relative.

Universal Mind, as compared with individual mind, is

synonymous with our absolute nature, whereas the individual mind is synonymous with our local, relative mind. Since the Absolute *is* the ultimate home and source of all, the relative must change, evolve, and eventually surrender its expression in time and space and return to its source.

An ice crystal may temporarily identify with its present form, enjoying its hardness and color, but it will eventually melt into liquid, taking on a new form and a new name. Eventually, as it is *bound to change*, the water evaporates into the expansiveness of gas and the gas disassociates into its base elements. Similarly, our soul takes on form, experiences the relative world of change so that we may release our karmic memories and return to our eternal, absolute source, the unity of God. Before our soul's journey is complete, it is possible to bridge the gap between our illusory, relative world and the ultimate, unbounded reality of the absolute. Our experience of transcendence becomes a reminder of the truth, inspiring us with the knowledge of the transcendental, helping us release the attachments to form and expand beyond its limits.

Our Higher Self, being a purely symbolic manifestation of the God-within, can assume any form and communicate with us in countless ways. Usually it comes to us in a form that is compatible with our belief system, a form that we may have been devoted to in the past. Our Higher Self may also bring us spiritual guides or other souls with whom we have a relationship (whether incarnate or not) or souls who have heard our calls and prayers.

In this life, it seems my Methodist background was not exciting enough spiritually, so even before I understood what was happening, Krishna began to appear to me. When I started to truly work on myself spiritually, Krishna was my constant companion, coaching me through my most difficult karmic themes and teaching me about life.

Recently, Krishna taught me a valuable lesson about

communication. I was working in my garden one afternoon. It was routine work and I was having an enjoyable and productive day. Then I noticed a pain under my right rib-cage in what felt like my liver. I tried to ignore it, but it just kept getting worse. Within fifteen minutes, I collapsed to the ground, curled up in the fetal position, and groaned in agony. There was nobody around to help me, but I finally reached the house. I couldn't figure out what was happening. The pain continued and began to spread down my body. All I could do was scream. It had happened so suddenly that it scared me "out of my mind." The torture continued for about two hours until I was exhausted and just wanted to die. I had tried everything I knew but nothing worked. After continually asking my Higher Self what to do, begging for the pain to go away, I finally gave up.

Then, unexpectedly, I heard a chant inside my head, "Shri Ram, Jai Jai Ram." I knew it was part of a Rama/Krishna chant, but it was one that I knew only vaguely. The chant seemed to go on by itself, as if someone was singing it *to* me, inside my head. Even more remarkable is that in less than a minute, all the pain was gone! I lay there in a state of awe, disbelieving this miracle and how it occurred. In place of the pain was a silent peace. My agonized tossing and turning was now a stillness accompanied by the feeling of a peaceful presence. I felt Krishna there, holding me in a mist of bluish radiance. After some time of resting, I stood up and felt my body. It felt normal, as if nothing had happened. The chant had been the key that released my pain. Asking, begging, and demanding were not my answers; only my surrendering worked. My past experiences, some as amazing as this one, had already proven the reality of God's presence. However, in the trauma of my pain, I had forgotten. The mantra resonating in my consciousness had delivered me back to the energy of my beloved, which opened me to peace once again. I realized once again how the emotional body tests us with pain so that we may find God even then. Surrender, faith, and trust are all components of opening blocked communication in order to transcend obstacles.

The Nature of Reality

Before we look at one form of spiritual communication, we must discuss a theory of the nature of reality. The absolute pure being is an unbounded, eternally silent field of pure consciousness. It is unchangeable, yet it is a field of pure potential, the source of all manifest creation. All energy and matter of the manifest universes arise from across the "dividing line" of unmanifest to the manifest. For lack of a better word, I will call this dividing line "the gap" because the experience of transcendence takes us through subtler and subtler levels until we bridge the gap into unbounded awareness. At that transition point there is still the sensing of something yet it is completely abstract.

In one interpretation of Hinduism, the gap between the relative world of form and the absolute world of formlessness is the realm of *Vishnu*, the subtlest celestial form of God. The Creator, *Brahma*, exists further into relativity because of the nature of manifestation; and *Shiva*, the Dissolver/Destroyer, absorbs creation back into the unmanifest. Vishnu sits in the eternal moment of the gap, maintaining both the absolute and the relative, yet permitting us a divine form to relate to before we enter into his omnipresent unity.

Our life is a path in which we experience creation by separating from God, by entering into form, and by enduring the illusion of change with all its myriad lifetimes and karmic lessons. We are born, grow old, and die over and over again until we surrender to the eternal moment of divine love and enter the gap to experience Vishnu. It is only he who takes us across the threshold to our home in Brahman, the absolute. The doorway is the moment, the password is Love, and the homecoming gift is the experience of divinity.

In Hinduism there are three forces within nature, the *Trimurti*, which are the archetypes of Brahma, the Creator; Vishnu, the Maintainer; and Shiva, the Destroyer. These forces or laws of nature can be located in any phenomena because collectively it is they that support evolution. The flower opens with the creative urge to blossom, sharing its splendor and sweet scent for a time, maintaining its perfection before releasing itself and its seeds for new life to spring forth. Without dissolution there can be no creation, and without creation nothing will continue. At each stage, something supports the flow and maintains each step of life.

That which preserves the unmanifest and the manifest, the silent and the active, is truly magnificent. Creation and destruction within life are expressed through time, but what is expressed when the illusion of time is removed? If there is no time, the flower does not blossom and the scent does not fade. No time means no change; only the moment remains. Vishnu comes forward, the archetype of the eternal now, and teaches us the contentment of the here and now—how to be completely at home in the everlasting Self. But prior to our enlightenment and during the expansion of our consciousness, he instills within us the instinct of self-preservation in order to maintain our desire for the infinity of God. Vishnu supports us in our longing for perfection as we travel through time to his realm of timelessness.

The name Vishnu comes from the Sanskrit root *vish*, which means "to enter." Thus life-force *enters* into form and the soul dons a body as part of the journey through illusion. Vishnu preserves and supports us along the path until we shed the illusion and *enter* into his reality as Brahman. Entering

Brahman, we become Brahman. Entering the absolute, we realize the absolute.

Krishna, regarded as the eighth incarnation of Vishnu, says in the *Bhagavad Gita*, "... keep me near, at every moment; trust me with your life, because I am you, more than you yourself are." The symbol of Vishnu is best expressed by the incarnation of Krishna, who supposedly lived 5,000 years ago, and then again as Siddhartha, the Buddha, 2,5000 years ago. Both incarnations teach of the Self and transcending the illusions of the material world.

Krishna is one of the most unique religious figures. Historically, it is uncertain whether or not he actually lived in physical body but regardless, he is cherished by a large part of the human race. He was considered by many to be an avatar (an incarnation of God) who chose to incarnate at a time of spiritual collapse in order to set humanity back on the path of dharma (spiritual consciousness) and rekindle the knowledge of the Ultimate Reality. He is the main character of the *Bhagavad-Gita*, that jewel of timeless wisdom that Hindus consider to be their bible. Strange to most Westerners, Krishna was the Divine Lover, known to enchant women, teaching love and having an erotically good time at it. I see Krishna as one of the best expressions of the Divine Child, full of the joy of the cosmic joke. He may have been a vital political and social activist, but he knew how to play and celebrate the divinity of life in this world and beyond. That Divine Child aspect allowed him to see beyond the drama of life which he is constantly reminding us of. For me, Krishna is real. But of course I can hear him laughing at my ignorance even now!

The following session exemplifies the rich symbolism of the Krishna archetype.

A Session with Krishna

All I see is a deep, flawless cobalt blue color, all pervasive. I know this color; it is the aura of Krishna—Krishna blue. He's now standing on my right, appearing androgynous, a young man smiling.

He returns me to a God experience I had a few months ago outside of Melbourne, Australia. The experience lasted 12 hours and I processed every relationship in my life with such love and forgiveness. He says I was using his loving Krishna energy. I didn't know it at the time, but now I know... (Tears)

He shows me my past roles in service to this galaxy and, recently, to this planet—a helping, healing role. It's energetic, a flow of light; but I got stuck, so absorbed in the "stuff," the polarities of this dimension. It pulled me into human body. I fight the density; I try really hard to disengage. The more I struggle, the more deeply attached I become. I feel desperate. I'm losing my power. But I also see that I'm still connected with the Krishna energy... (Body relaxes)

I'm asking him what I should do. He says, "I never answer a question twice." He doesn't give the same answer twice so I must already know what to do!

He's maneuvering me between the relative world and the Absolute. All I feel is a tremendous pulsating vibration; it permeates me. In one direction, I see a shimmering light; it's matter and energy being created. In the other direction, there is darkness, but it's as if I could perceive the stillness, the unmanifest Being. I'm in the gap, the boundary between that which is nothingness, but it's so full... and this world of change. Here, in this gap, I feel eternity, never ending, just pure consciousness, pure love; yet I still have thoughts and feelings but I'm not those feelings. I'm love but not in love—so open. It's incredible! It's a point of the "maintaining" I see. It's the residence of Vishnu! Krishna has brought me here to see him, to know him in his universal form. I feel so touched. I feel my friend, my god, my personality opening into universality. I wish I had words.... (Silence)

I feel my healing crystal pulsating in my hand. It's being programmed, coded with this knowing. In this place there is constancy, eternal support—a sanctuary of refuge. No matter what I do, any activity, any chore, my witness aspect is infused and preserved with this energy—eternally there.

The eternal aspect is only a bridge into the Absolute. The eternal has meaning only here in the gap; in the Absolute there is no meaning—it has no function, but to Be. So full, so full....

I see the creative aspect manifest out of the Absolute silence and the destructive aspect takes creation back into the Absolute. Krishna is more subtle because he supports and preserves this whole process; without him, there would be no creation, growth, or dissolution.

He says, "Come unto me; I am the gateway." He is the technique, the pathway. I need to go deeper into this.... (Silence)

The Bhakti yogi [the technique of devotion as a path to Enlightenment] *gets attached here. They don't want to move across the gap; they just stay on the edge, eternally in love. They want to feel the energetic quality of love as it bridges into the absolute, to feel it, but not take the step across the gap. They're so in love with Krishna, they don't want to give it up. Because Krishna is eternal they think that it's infinity, but it's not the final step....*

Krishna says, "There is still attachment to the illusion of time. When you are ready to take the step, I am here to help you."

I feel a merging of my human heart with his divine heart; it happens here in the gap. All have to pass through this, some more quickly than others. Buddha demonstrated how if attached to nothing, not even to God, you may pass through quickly. The Bhakta has lessons to learn there with Krishna.

Krishna laughs. He turns into a Divine Child still laughing and he says, "Does this form remind you of anything?"

Somehow I never got the point of what that was all about, until now. Krishna is certainly a patient teacher!

I see a triangle with its base at the top and the point down. Left is Divine Mother, right is Divine Father, and below is the Divine Child. The Divine Child is central to the balance between Yin and Yang, the fusion of polarity into Oneness. Vishnu/Krishna is certainly the center of the Male and Female, Creator and Destroyer—the androgynous one who holds it all together. The Krishna Child is so symbolic; it sends thrills of bliss through my body.

My path is predetermined. (Silence)

The heart chakra will open in relation to Krishna. The throat chakra is the gap, communication the key that opens the door, and the third eye opens with that realization.

I had lost it. Now this experience has re-awakened me from my sleep. I feel the clarity of mind of Krishna, the joy of the eternal moment in the heart of Krishna. Both are my path. His body is the gap. He says to do the practices; time doesn't exist so don't worry about result. Do the practices, and move into relationship with Krishna in my being.

There's just cobalt blue; it permeates. It's so profound. Why are words so limited? It's so intense. My heart is blue cobalt vibration. Krishna says that not everybody's chakras are the same color. I always knew that my heart chakra is blue, not green.

He also says to write the book. In the gap, communication, that flow of energy and intelligence, fuses into the experience of communion where both aspects exist simultaneously. On one side, the relative side, the energy is of crystal clarity, perfect in form and content; in the middle of the gap, the energy moves into perfect balance, preserved for eternity yet full of potential; and on the absolute side, the energy produces communion with the source, unified, fulfilled in its completion. (Silence)

(Tears) *After all of this, I still worry about losing it like I did before. Like Arjuna on the battlefield. After the battle, I see a boy asking Krishna what he told Arjuna on the battlefield. Krishna says that he told him the secret of life, but he has already forgotten. We forget but we also remember. Every time even one of us remembers, the world remembers, and it lasts a little longer. The lesson is learned a bit better. The light shines deeper into the darkness of our ignorance. If the candle goes out, we just light it once again. Don't worry, just do what you have to do.*

It's so incredible, my mind just has to let go.... (Silence)
(End of session)

The Uses of Time:
Past, Present, and Future

Krishna is one of the master teachers about the illusion of time. He *symbolizes* the gateway to the transcendence of time and, therefore, the ability to live in the eternal moment. Past, present, and future, on the level of the subtle, are not divided by time but are each connected with and within the other.

What is important for us, living in a dimension of time, is to feel the flow of the present in the past and the future. The present is all-important because it provides us with the ability to make choices, to change, and to envision the evolution the future brings.

Unfortunately, the past carries with it the stigma of pain and regret, all the difficult lessons of life to which we are still attached in the present and which propel us forward into the future. The past holds us in the grip of its unresolved karma. Another way to say this is that *the past demands we learn the lessons before we graduate into the liberation of the eternal present*—only then do past and future disappear *energetically* within our consciousness. The liberated present has captured unboundedness; time is no longer a factor in our life equation.

For most of us, the past demands our attention; it carries the lessons that give us keys to our present and future. We cannot afford to forget the past; in fact, we must use the present to heal the past, to let it go, to free ourselves from its grip. In the present, we can take our consciousness into the past and change it. On the level of spirit, our multidimensional consciousness has the ability to reprogram the past, to create a "feedback loop" that touches the clouds of pain and ignorance and recreates with the nonjudgmental wisdom of the Higher Self.

In the psychospiritual session work of the Deva Foundation, the facilitator helps the client to move inside, into his or her unconscious. Moving beyond time into the energy of the karmic attachments, our Higher Self helps us to release the grip of our past karma and in essence, to transmute what has been judged as a transgression or mistake into the perfection of the path. Our Higher Self then gives us the wisdom from its teaching so we are able to feel the balance of past, present, and future.

This process evolves in our consciousness until the present moment liberates the future through the releasing of our illusion of fear. Fear is future oriented and the freedom of the present, now based in nonattachment to the past, clears all fear and brings us face to face with God, our Creator, and through grace, allows our heart to expand with the onrush of love. As this spiritual energy flows up into the throat chakra, it releases the last remnants of judgment that have separated us from the Divine. Our individuality melts away into a merging, and our personal consciousness becomes the infinite consciousness. The past, present, and future are thus unified into the oneness.

Realities Beyond Security and Fear

How conservative we all are! Prisoners of the familiar, demanding others to see the world as we do, to behave as we do. We require the masses to conform to the rigors of civilization, and we threaten them with judgment if they do not. Here we have the paradox of communication: in order to communicate, we require some degree of a common "language." We also mix in a certain expectation of behavior and an anticipation of a desired response. The cauldron bubbles and experience serves us a dish, rich in sensory data, and ready for *the* response. If all goes well, our response is simple and direct. But if the ingredients presented to us are unfamiliar, unexpected, or confusing, the weight of the painful past may shut us down into withdrawal or separation. In this case, communication has not so much failed as it has triggered an emotional state that doesn't allow for connection, much less understanding. This predicament is reinforced by the need for "normalcy," order, and the requirement of our culture that we "think and act" as one. So we create the artist, who is given license to "be different." We feel if everyone were different, chaos would ensnare us in its unpredictability.

The only solution must include freedom from judgment, openness to innovation or new perspectives on living, and the releasing of any self-righteous need to have it "my way." Experimentation may lead to preferences, yet we don't need to project them onto society. Releasing control is certainly a challenge, but "going with the flow" is a novelty whose time has come. Conservatism may embody wisdom from the past, but part of that wisdom is how to turn opportunity into beneficial change, allowing growth and expression of deeper realms to manifest into power and prosperity. Our emotional tendency is to habituate, to make life routine in order to give us a sense of security. If this is taken too far, we stagnate in our over-familiarity, and life's potential is branded with fear, imprinted for the future.

Our addiction to speed and to drugs that dissolve our inhibitions and give the rush of greater potential are calling our attention to a world where our lives are stagnant, held in the grip of fear. The message is clear: life holds more for us than we live; our senses want to expand as our consciousness expands. Expansion brings us back to the spiritual, to that commonality that connects everything together. With expansion, the emptiness of fragmentation is filled from another level—from something we thought was gone but that has just been waiting for us to open the door. Communication with its omnipresent potential will help us rediscover the unity that brings us into communion.

Devotion—The Path of Love

Often we hear catchy phrases such as "You create your own reality," "Life is but a game," and "Life is in unity; we are One." These are common truths for the spiritual seeker. If we asked their meaning we would probably hear simple, legitimate answers to satisfy our inquiry. Yet for most of us, the answers are still coming from our intellect—on deeper levels we just don't get it! We're victims of "heart bypass." Our intellect keeps us from feeling the truth and living its profundity on cellular and cosmic levels. We may *think* that we create our own reality, but we haven't gone deep enough, beyond causation. We may still believe that the reason relationships fail is because of our parents' divorce or our father's anger or our first lover's unkindness. We hear "life is but a game," and we are trapped in it. We agree to play by the rules and get angry or judgmental if others do not play by them to our satisfaction. We get confused if we attempt to play it otherwise. The rule of cause and effect still holds us tightly, unforgiving, like a referee that demands the game be played correctly. The rules, our roles, and our expectations of what may happen structure our game of life and reality as we play. This is not only true on the material plane but also on subtler planes of creation.

To create our reality assumes many things. First, it assumes we have the ability to create, the power of will that can structure material life. Does God create our life, observe us and end it if s/he doesn't like what we are doing? Is it like building an ant farm, putting the ants in it, and watching them play until we decide to destroy it? Are we ants solely under the Creator's control? Or do we, as the creators of our own reality, use our innate divinity as our source of creativity?

Our personal creation has as its source the nonlocal, pure intelligence that we call God. Therefore, our creation is not separate from God, but is an expression of God's infinite possibility. Our limitation is that we also create judgment, which obscures the grand perfection of all things. Judgment creates rules, roles, and demands in the game of life. Judgment makes the game difficult; it takes the fun out of it. It is our themes of separation/judgment that turn our life into a chore. Separation/judgment is part of *our own* creation. Although we may have projected this role onto God, it is this role that has created the polarity and karma of the game of cause and effect. In order to change our reality, we must penetrate deep into the fabric of our memory and untie those fundamental knots that have structured the illusion of our separation from the divine. The "judgment knot" is old and *seems* resistant to our attempts to untie it, but if we believe it is possible, the knot will dissolve and the fabric of our illusion will unravel into nothingness.

The concept of God is one of ultimate wisdom, infinite intelligence, unbounded love, omnipotent, and omnipresent. The Creator, Maintainer, and Destroyer of life, eternally unified in the present, is always available. If we have the ability to create or co-create our personal reality then why not create from this concept of God? The game of life would then have as its basis wisdom, intelligence, love, and omnipotence. Our reality is full of these divine attributes, regardless of the appearance of their polar opposites in the tragicomedy of life. And in the final scene, the negativities become transparent and release their illusion of power and control. Eventually the polarities dissolve back into the simple reality of God's perfection—the veil of ignorance has been lifted once again and the game has been transcended. We can choose to play or not; we are the creator of the game and, if we wish, we can change the rules. Being the master of our own destiny, we are solely responsible.

Responsibility is a part of the game. Every creator is responsible for his or her own creation. Yet we are so adept at projecting blame and seeing cause as external that we lose the power to change. Every time we blame another, we give away our power and "create" ourselves as the victim. Taking responsibility empowers us and refines our ability to create. On a personal level, we learn from experience, both from our actions and the actions of others. When judgment is released, responsibility is simple and easy—as well as learning and change.

As I discussed earlier, judgment makes the process difficult. Letting it go can be as hard as realizing its presence in every thought, word, and deed. Living in the energy of separation is like being inside a bubble looking out: it is so familiar that we do not even notice it. Even when we finally recognize it, the challenge to heal it is only just beginning. The solution is not psychological; *it can only be spiritual*. The experience of the Divine prepares the way of the heart. Love heals judgment but it is not enough to love only momentarily because *the cessation of love returns us to separation*. Only perpetual love is the answer. This becomes the path of devotion.

Devotion is the selfless expression of the love of God. If God is love, then my giving love is the giving of God back to God. If God is within me, then loving God is loving myself. Devoting myself to God is devoting myself to the God within and around me.

The key word is *selfless*. Selfless devotion does not mean we indulge our ego or go around telling everyone that we are God. To be selfless is to transcend the personal self into the transpersonal self. By recognizing our omnipresent self, communion becomes possible. The merging opens us to the ecstasy of Love—God loving God through the infinite variety of form. Devotion is the return to communion. It can add a new dimension to our communication with the universe of divinity.

Since the ego holds most of us so tightly, devotion usually begins by externalizing our attention toward something that we love. It may be a religious symbol like a cross, a picture of a guru or even the embodiment of the Divine Mother herself. A good example is seen in the writing of Andrew Harvey as he discusses his experiences of devotion to Mother Meera in his book *The Hidden Journey*.

Devotion doesn't have to be religious; it can be very personal and close to home. The love shared by a husband and wife, by committed partners, or by a teacher and student can be put on the pedestal of devotion. My guru's love for his teacher was an incredible example of love and surrender. But watching the devotion of many others has never quite equaled the devotional experience with which I have been blessed from my wife, Paula Rachel Kaufman.

In Rachel, I often sense the Divine Mother. Although she has an emotional body that hurts at times, it is just emotional energy passing through—a mask, a role that is playing itself out. In reality, it isn't God that steps *in*, it is the ego that steps *out,* revealing the God that has always been there. As Rachel practices her devotion, she practices stepping out of her ego, taking off the mask, exiting the stage where the dramas are acted out. She practices love and new ways to express it. The new mask is transparent and reveals her true self underneath. The new role is about new ways of expressing kindness, compassion, and understanding. Through her practicing a new way of being, her life of devotion exemplifies and stimulates within *me* a resonance of attraction to her, to me, and to the God that links us both. I learn, she teaches; she learns, I teach. Our new game of devotional communication empowers us both with the love of God.

In order for it to work, it requires that each of us release our self-judgment, for this alone keeps our hearts closed—feeling that we were undeserving of the love of God. Having been separated from God when we first came into form, we internalized alienation and aloneness, creating the fertile ground of judgment. Our divine heart was imprisoned, love was restricted, and issues of worthiness came into play. The ability to know God, to commune in oneness, was but a distant dream. Devotion can make the dream a reality. *We are the creators and we can rewrite the script.* To create the lover is a glorious creation.

Let my prayer resonate: God help us embrace Divine Love, to treasure it, to let it heal all wounds. Let my consciousness envelop the lover as God. When I see the Buddha sitting in communion, let it remind me of my own Buddhahood, so I may live in the infinite openness of unity.

The Drama of Suffering

The most intense drama of life is the drama of suffering. Our world is filled with it. We have played a role in it many times. It is a role of seeking more and more, but finding only incompleteness and unfulfillment. The role is ancient; the behavior habituated. The desperate striving for even a moment of happiness and peace can be seen in the drug addict who takes a drug yet knows full well the consequences. An addict knows desire and its resulting trade-off better than most. But those moments of no pain, the cherished feeling of peace and ease, are all that we really want. The game of life is also about impermanence. Desire and gratification are only transitory. Happiness and pain alternate in their momentary, polarized extremes. As long as the pendulum swings, equanimity is impossible; the middle road escapes our attempts to find balance.

Yet stability does not mean that we lock ourselves into some numbed-out, neutral state of feeling. Whether there is pain or pleasure, the awareness of Self is always available. This and only this awareness provides balance. Enlightenment is that state of life where we disengage and liberate ourselves from the swing of the pendulum. Though it may swing, we are no longer attached to its movement; we are established in our center. Free from the grip of suffering or transitory pleasure, we rest in our self-effulgent peace. No longer do we seek happiness outside because we are filled inside. No longer do we avoid pain because it can not overshadow our inner bliss.

The ecstatic state of enlightenment is not yet realized for most of us so we try to emulate it, conjure it, and control our behavior in attempts to make it real. This is like playing a role from our head rather than knowing it in our heart. There are many "spiritual" teachers who play their role brilliantly but it remains a role missing in its vital essence. Our path may require us to keep rehearsing while the heart opens. Our real challenge is of the heart.

The Tao of a New Millennium

Our old pattern of seeking fulfillment through the grabbing of pleasure and the addiction to impermanence has created a narcissistic approach to life, and thus a collapse into the aloneness and pain of separation. The fight for survival has put us all into constant competition, where even the family has disintegrated.

The new way, *the Tao of a New Millennium,* offers a solution to our unfulfilled state of existence. Our new environmental awareness has profoundly reminded us that our planet is home to all of us. Instead of a consciousness of divisiveness where people strive for nationalism, protectionism, and all the other "ism's" of separation, we are now witnessing an opening of dialogue, of free trade, of a united approach to the global issues that touch each resident of this planet, our common home. New means of communication give us the opportunity to share the energies that bring us into more intimate contact. In essence, it is a spiritual manifestation of our innate oneness.

This way of a new beginning must include a choice to reach out, to share resources, and to help each other. In order to reach out we must improve our ability to communicate. And instead of being addicted to unfulfillment, scarcity and pain, we must provide the necessities of life—adequate food, unpolluted water and air, proper shelter, and, most importantly, compassion, which gives hope to the spirit. In other words, we must open our economic resources and our hearts to serve humanity and through the power of human loving kindness, we can then serve Mother Earth.

The history of competition which creates winners and losers—the polarities of separation—is gradually lifting from our collective consciousness. The manipulation of life for our immediate gratification—oblivious to our children's future—has brought us to the crossroads of our planet's survival. We have a collective choice that will create the next chapter of our human reality. We can continue to live in a world of judgment and separation, seeing ourselves as individuals competing for survival, or we can choose to see ourselves as one—one family sharing life in a shared world, where judgment is released into permission, into love and compassion, where separation dissolves into the unity of all things. From this comes our inherent expression of giving. Service to others becomes the norm.

We can see this occurring throughout the world already. As the powers of greed and separation disintegrate, wisdom will give rise to serving ourselves by serving others. Charity will no longer be seen as something that is given to the less fortunate, but as an energy of love and caring that fulfills the giver in the process of giving. Obviously, communication is fundamental and will become multidimensionally effective as the new way—of the nineties and thereafter. Its success will bring us into communion, and then we shall know God.

Conclusion

I never imagined that I would write a book, much less two of them. But I found that writing about my inner thoughts and feelings was an effective processing technique. As I communicate outwardly to the printed page, my thoughts clarify themselves. Writing has given my living reality a new degree of consciousness, allowing me to perceive the inner process of my clients and the world around me more deeply.

While writing this book, my Higher Self seemed to bless me with experiences that not only took me deeper into the themes of my exploration, but also confirmed my growth and opened new levels of awareness to life.

In the preface, I talked about the beginning of this sojourn into the realms of communication and the throat chakra. My dolphin friends gave me the touch of healing with their nonjudgmental transmission of freedom. Being pulled into their galactic consciousness, being imprinted with their love and joy, my heart merged with them in an energy of devotion that has enriched my life. This book arose from that experience and, as a result, has helped me to fulfill one of my life's challenges. As if my Higher Self wanted to reward me for my determination and success, the dolphins brought me yet another heartfelt gift.

After working intensely in Australia and Indonesia in the Spring of 1991, Rachel and I returned to a Hawaiian sanctuary on the north shore of Kauai to spend time resting and reflecting. A year and a half before, in this very place, the dolphins had initiated me into their world. Many mornings we would watch them play as they spun out of the water, splashing each other in their joy. We always reveled in their excitement, and I would feel those sacred moments flood back into my body when I was with them.

One late afternoon, I heard Rachel call from the porch that

overlooks thousands of miles of ocean and I knew our friends were back. As I left my writing to see the dolphins, I felt a *new* excitement. This was somehow different from the countless other times we watched the dolphins appear. As I scanned the horizon, I saw their unmistakable splash. Then Rachel said, "Do you think that you could swim all the way out there?"

Realizing that it was about a mile, perhaps much more, I understood what she was asking. The amount of time it would take for me to swim that far seemed to be futile; the dolphins would surely be long gone by then. But my Higher Self, with its familiar clarity, said, "Do it!"

Within seconds, I had stripped down to my underwear and was dashing into the water with my fins and mask. As a former competitive swimmer, I felt a familiar rhythm and an almost forgotten, youthful power flow through my body. It felt good to fly through the water, and within minutes I could no longer see the bottom. I realized I was swimming in the center of the world's largest ocean toward the Aleutian Islands. But it seemed just another boundary to transcend. Although my *mind* knew I was getting tired, my *body* denied all fear.

Then, underwater, I heard the dolphins' call. My breathing was so loud and forceful that I had to stop to listen; there it was, the unmistakable whistles of the dolphins. I looked toward the shore where Rachel was standing to point out the direction of the dolphins, but I was too far away, I couldn't see her anymore. I decided to follow my intuition, so I went under again and swam like a racer into the unknown.

After some time, I became worried that I was getting too far away from shore. My mind reminded me of ocean currents, cramps, and all the chatterings of caution, but I let it go because inside I knew I was getting close. The dolphins' calls were stronger now, the energy drawing me on. Then something told me to quit swimming and look around. The moment I pulled my head up, three dolphins jumped about twenty-five meters behind me, as if to say, "Here we are!"

Rachel later told me that I was swimming at an angle away from the dolphins; but because they knew I was coming and realized that as a human, my navigation skills were terribly lacking, they changed direction and swam after me. She saw them surround me as I stopped. And then, as Rachel danced with joy, the dolphins started their acrobatic show for me.

Within seconds, I was surrounded by about thirty dolphins. I thought my heart would explode with joy. They swam under me, brushing against my legs. They jumped over me. They swam directly at me and then divided at the last moment to pass me on each side. A couple swam stomach to stomach in their mating posture as the symbol of their loving connection with me. My consciousness was taking in all their multidimensional messages.

Then, as if to sober me up, they gave me a powerful splash in the face, and we would swim in circles together.

At one point, there were twenty dolphins swimming in a tight circle around me. The spiral of energy created a vortex that seemed to carry me into the galaxies, yet my body was completely anchored to Earth via the water element. The ocean's essence seemed to resonate to the psycho-biochemical nature of all life forms, creating a universal bond of unity. My consciousness was working on so many different levels that I could witness the symbolic significance of this experience. But the greatest gift of all was the sharing of the bond of joy. I knew that healing through joy was what the world needed most—that transcendental explosion of the heart into the One Heart.

Finally, after about forty minutes of play, my body collapsed in ecstatic exhaustion, and I said good-bye to my dear friends and teachers. Realizing that I was far out in the middle of the ocean, I just floated for a while to catch my breath, and leisurely, I started my long but blissful swim back to land to share the experience with my favorite human. I didn't feel like I was the same person. A transformation had taken place. All I wanted was to bring a new message to the world: a message of unity, of communion in Spirit.

As I stepped on shore, I saw Rachel's tears of happiness. There was such gratitude in her eyes. Then she pointed to the sky. Arching over the house and mountains was a double rainbow, complete in its grandeur. I fell into her arms, and we cried together in joy.

About the Author

Rick Phillips, author of *Emergence of the Divine Child*, is a teacher and psychospiritual facilitator for the work of the Deva Foundation, of which he and his wife, Paula Rachel Kaufman, are cofounders. Rick and Rachel travel all over the world, working with individuals, offering lectures and workshops on themes of personal and planetary healing, including their well-known *Heart Retreat*. In addition, they devote much of their time to developing the charitable aspect of the Deva Foundation in its role of service and social action for the planet.

Rick and Rachel live in the mountains near Santa Fe, New Mexico. To contact them or to receive more information about the Deva Foundation, please write or call:

Deva Foundation
P.O. Box 309
Glorieta, New Mexico 87535
USA

Tel. and Fax: (505)757-6752
E-Mail: Rick Phillips/Rachel Kaufman,
102465,2707@compuserve.com
Our World Wide Web Page
Address on the Internet is:
http://www.deva.org

REFERENCES

Chapter 2

1. Larry Dossey, <u>Recovering the Soul</u>. (New York, Bantam Books, 1989), p.166.

Chapter 6

1. W. Y. Evans-Wentz, <u>Tibetan Book of the Dead</u>. (London, Oxford University Press, 1960), pp.165-168.

2. T. Leary, R. Metzer, and R. Alpert, <u>Psychedelic Experience</u>. (New York, Citadel Press, 1964), pp. 87-88.

3. Aldous Huxley, <u>The Perennial Philosophy</u>. (New York, Harper and Row, 1944), p. 229.

4. Larry Dossey, <u>Recovering the Soul</u>. (New York, Bantam Books, 1989), pp. 268-269.

5. Ibid., p. 244.

6. Rick Phillips.

7. Ibid.

8. Kenneth Ring, <u>The Omega Project</u>. (New York, William Morrow and Co., 1992), p. 103.

9. Ibid., pp. 104-105

10. Ibid., p.104.

Chapter 7

1. W.Y. Evans-Wentz, <u>Tibetan Book of the Dead</u>. (London, Oxford University Press, 1960), p. 174

2. T. Leary, R. Metzer, and R. Alpert, <u>Psychedelic Experience</u>. (New York, Citadel Press, 1964), p. 12